Blueprint: New Testament Strategies for Building, Growing & Sustaining the Church

by Dr. Alphonso Scott

Published by HigherLife Publishing and Marketing
P.O. Box 623307
Oviedo, Florida 32762
(407) 563-4806
www.ahigherlife.com

ISBN hardback: 978-0-9978018-9-7

ISBN e-book: 978-0-9989773-2-4

Printed in the United States of America

BLUEPRINT

NEW TESTAMENT
STRATEGIES FOR
BUILDING,
GROWING &
SUSTAINING
THE CHURCH

BISHOP ALPHONSO SCOTT

"And I say also unto thee, that though art Peter, and upon this rock I will build my church, and the gates of hell shall not prevail against it."

—Matthew 16:18

Dedication

This book is dedicated to my father, the late Bishop Phillip L. Scott; my mother, Louvenia Scott; and my wife, Phyllis—all faithful warriors of Jesus Christ.

Table of Contents

Preface

Through my decades of church service, I have seen churches vary wildly in their approaches to the church: building churches, conducting church services, providing resources to the community, and worshipping the Lord.

In terms of the building itself, some church groups erect elaborate, ostentatious buildings that can cause members to wonder what their tithes are supporting, while others throw together unattractive buildings that are not inviting and cause people to question how devoted the leadership is to building a vibrant church. Neither way is best.

As for the services themselves, some churches focus too much on form, conducting elaborate rituals that can seem burdensome and archaic, while others focus on form too little, conducting casual church services that can seem irreverent.

And finally, when it comes to serving the community, some churches focus only on people's spiritual needs and neglect their physical and social needs. Others go to the other extreme, ministering to people's physical and social needs while focusing too little on the spiritual ones. In all of this, we need a balance.

If church leaders and members understood God's original purpose for the church, it could make it easier to establish and operate churches in a way *that meets God's expectations and people's needs in a biblically sound manner.* This book was written as a guidebook for church leaders and members to follow to reach this goal. Each chapter is focused on a particular aspect of the church and is followed by study questions. These questions when done in a group setting are intended to engender discussion and further growth.

It is important that church leaders and members alike take the care of the body of Christ seriously. This book can help church leaders achieve the right balance of reverence and spontaneity so that we can attract and retain members who are committed to furthering the work of Jesus Christ. It will also help us build strong churches that serve as the divine agency for promoting and extending the Lord's kingdom.

"Let us therefore follow after the things which make for peace, and things wherewith one may edify another" (Romans 14:19).

Introduction

Although the church had its roots in the Old Testament, it is chiefly a New Testament institution. It is in the New Testament that we find the origin, pattern, mission, and early history of the church.

Using the New Testament as a guide and primary source for its narrative, this book focuses on the New Testament church—its beginning, growth, nature, government, leaders, ordinances, worship, work, and triumph. The following are just a few of the many topics this book studies:

- How six of the first and most important churches in history were established through the Roman Empire, and by whom

- How God intended the church to be designed and governed

- The unique nature of the church

- God's expectation of how members are to worship, observe ordinances, and serve the community

- How the offices of elder and deacon were designed to serve the church body

- The purposes and various parts of worship

As we examine the origin and growth of the early churches, we begin to appreciate how the church has survived centuries of turmoil and persecution. Even though the church has always faced the enemies of unbelief, covetousness, worldliness, and formalism, it will triumph in the end. Each time the church seems to be on the verge of destruction, it emerges with new life and power. Jesus is mighty in His church!

When we join together as families, committed to preparing for His return by praying diligently and sincerely for all people, we are building churches that worship Him, minister to people's needs, provide a place of fellowship, teach others about His Word, and spread His gospel throughout the world. We are building according to the blueprint He gave us.

Dr. Alphonso Scott

Foreword

Blueprint is a comprehensive and yet detailed work that speaks to the heart of the life of the church in this present day. It reveals the church as an historical institution that is being challenged but has weathered every storm and is still recognized as a relevant and vibrant voice speaking to humanity today. Blueprint is required reading for pastors and members as well as academicians who are looking to understand the purpose for the church in light of biblical truth.

This is a profound work that takes a hard look at what the church has become while reminding the reader of the initial reason for its existence: The church is not just another entity in our world, but must be taken serious because of its divine origin.

Dr. Alphonso Scott has produced a work that presents a realistic view of church history while, at the same time, revealing the unique connection between the Old Testament and the New Testament worship. The author makes it evident that the church has survived centuries of turmoil and persecution and yet remains the true cornerstone of society today. This work does not attempt to present the church as perfect. In contrast, the author invites the reader to see the church as the representation of the kingdom of heaven in the earth.

Blueprint provides insight, revealing the church as not just a natural building but as a spiritual and living organization that portrays a group of people committed to being a witness of the love of God for mankind. This book covers every base and draws attention to the truth that the church's origin was and is divine. Although written from an academic perspective, it communicates biblical principles in a way that can be comprehended by all. The author drives home the point that the church was begun with design in mind. As a result, all believers must be committed to the work of the ministry as one.

Dr. Scott explores the mechanics of the church with passion and attempts to reveal to the reader how he or she can be a part of this established organization as they are called to minister to the needs of mankind. In this age, there is no greater need than for the church to realize its true identity and fulfill its divine mission. There is no message that is needed in the world today more than that of the church. Dr. Scott affirms that every individual, believer or not, will experience trials and suffer hardships. However, he trumpets the reality that one and all can experience triumph and know victory in the end.

This book is a must-read if the church is to understand the simple, time-tested and proven precepts that were meant to cause it to prosper. It speaks to leaders as well as the laity, and exposes the victories as well as the defeats. But more importantly, it is specifically focused on preparing every individual for the coming of the Lord while revealing what it takes to experience the hope that can only be found in relationship with the church.

Blueprint will open the eyes of everyone pursuing the truth concerning the church, its history, and its relevancy even today. This book has blessed me as a person, a pastor, and as a leader. I encourage you to take the time to read it and believe that you will be enlightened in your knowledge of the church, its purpose, and your reason for being as well when you do.

—Dr. Clarence V. Boyd, Jr.
Dean of Spiritual Formation at Oral Roberts University, Author,
Pastor, Mentor, and Founder of Revelations-Revealed Truth
Ministries

Chapter 1

Our Beginnings: "Upon This Rock!"

The Bible and the church stand together. With roots in the Old Testament, it is primarily a New Testament institution. It is in the New Testament that we find the origin, pattern, mission, and early history of the church.

This makes the New Testament the true handbook of the church. Manmade creeds should never be substituted for the authority of the New Testament. Most of the errors that have found their way into the church through the ages can be traced to a departure from, or misinterpretation of, the primary teachings of the New Testament. What does the Bible have to say about the church?

THE ORIGIN OF THE CHURCH

The word "church" is the English translation of the Greek word *ecclesia*[1] or *ekklesia*, from which we get the word "ecclesiastic" and other kindred words. Ecclesia is made up of two Greek words that

---

1   "Strongs's #1577: ekklesia - Greek/Hebrew Definitions - Bible Tools," Strongs's #1577: ekklesia - Greek/Hebrew Definitions - Bible Tools, accessed January 04, 2017, http://www. bibletools.org/index.cfm/fuseaction/Lexicon.show/ID/G1577/ekklesia.htm.

mean "called out." Among the Greeks, an ecclesia was an assembly of free citizens called out from their homes and places of business to give consideration to matters of public interest. This group of people discussed the needs of their community and made decisions about how those needs should be met as well as how their community should proceed as they considered the questions of their time. The disciples would have been familiar with this word and its cultural meaning. We find ecclesia used this way three times in Acts 19, where it is translated as assembly:

> **The New Testament Writers often took a word in common use and poured spiritual content into it.**

"For the assembly [ecclesia] was confused" (verse 32, addition mine).

"But if ye inquire anything concerning other matters, it shall be determined in a lawful assembly [ecclesia]" (verse 39, addition mine).

"And when he had thus spoken, he dismissed the assembly [ecclesia]" (verse 41, addition mine).

The Septuagint, which is a Greek translation of the Hebrew Old Testament, uses the word ecclesia to designate the congregation of Israel called together before the tabernacle during their wilderness wanderings too. It is used in this context many times. Stephen referred to the ecclesia of Israel in his defense before his accusers. Speaking of Moses, he said, *"This is he that was in the church [ecclesia] in the wilderness"* (Acts 7:38, addition mine).

2

Likewise Hebrews 2:12 says, *"I will declare thy name unto my brethren, in the midst of the church [ecclesia] will I sing praise unto thee"* (addition mine).

Ecclesia is used five times in the New Testament (the original Greek version), in which there is no reference to the church of Christ except as to an assembly called together for various purposes. The New Testament writers often took a word in common use and poured spiritual content into it. John did that with the word *logos*. And Jesus did it with the word *ecclesia*. He endowed it with spiritual significance.

Ecclesia, designating the church of Christ, is found 109 times in the New Testament. Christ first used it as recorded in Matthew 16:18: *"And upon this rock I will build my church…"* The emphasis on the pronoun "My" as in—"My *ecclesia*"—in contrast with the *ecclesia* of the Greeks and Jews sets it apart. Jesus used a term and an idea that the disciples and the people around Him already understood and then added a deeper layer of meaning to it, one that the disciples could literally build upon later.

No verses in the Scripture have been the subject of more controversy than these words of Jesus: *"And I say also unto thee, that thou art Peter, and upon this rock I will build my church"* (Matthew 16:18). What was the rock on which Christ was to build His church? Three answers have been given to this question. Let's look at each one in detail.

SOME THINK PETER WAS THE ROCK

This was (and is) the claim of the Roman Catholic Church. It teaches that Christ appointed Peter as His vicar on earth, that Peter was the founder of the church at Rome, the first of the popes, and the transmitter of special grace. A few years ago, one of the popes declared that the bones of Peter had been found beneath St. Peter's Basilica in Rome. This is highly doubtful.

All evangelical spirit-filled believers, of course, reject this claim. *There is no direct evidence in the New Testament that Peter was ever in Rome, and certainly the New Testament does not give him a place of preeminence among the apostles.* In the same chapter in which Jesus said, *"Thou art Peter, and upon this rock I will build my church,"* He also said, addressing Peter, *"Get thee behind me, Satan: thou art an offense unto me: for thou savorest not the things that be of God, but those that be of men"* (Matthew 16:23). Peter was also severely rebuked by the church at Antioch for hypocritical behavior much later (Galatians 2:11–12). And Peter made no claim of preeminence for himself. Instead he spoke of himself as a fellow elder. When he wrote to the churches, he addressed them thus: *"The elders which are among you I exhort, who am also an elder…"* (1 Peter 5:1). These are not the words of a man who considers himself as the leader of all. Peter never made any claim to be anything more than one of the Twelve. It really does not agree with the whole counsel of God to regard Peter as anything more than that.

But there are outstanding scholars who think that Jesus did not refer to Peter as the rock upon which He would build His church but rather referred to Peter as representing all who truly confess Christ as the divine Savior and Lord.

CHRIST AS THE ROCK

This interpretation is based on the fact that "rock" or "stone," as used in the Bible, almost invariably refers to God. Such passages include:

"For other foundation can no man lay than that is laid, which is Jesus Christ" (1 Corinthians 3:11).

"Ye also, as lively stones, are built up a spiritual house, an holy priesthood, to offer up spiritual sacrifices, acceptable to God by Jesus Christ" (1 Peter 2:5).

"Wherefore also it is contained in the scripture, Behold, I lay in Zion a chief corner stone, elect, precious: and he that believeth on him shall not be confounded" (1 Peter 2:6).

Professor Alfred E. Day, a Bible expositor from the Syrian Protestant College in Beirut, Lebanon, says this about the definition of "rock": "If we trace the figurative use of the word 'rock' throughout the Hebrew Scripture, we find it is never used symbolically of man, but always of God." Here at Caesarea Philippi as Jesus spoke with His disciples, it is not upon Peter that He plans to build His church. Jesus did not trifle with figures of speech. He took up the Old Hebrew illustration—rock, always the symbol of deity—and said, in essence, "Upon God Himself I will build My church. My kingdom shall consist of those who are built into God: those who are partakers of the divine nature." Jesus knew that all His followers were familiar with the Old Testament, in which the word "rock" refers to God over and over and over again. His disciples could not have missed such an obvious reference. Let's review just a few of these powerful references:

> # Jesus knew that all His followers were familiar with the Old Testament.

"He is the Rock, his work is perfect: for all his ways are judgment: a God of truth and without iniquity, just and right is he" (Deuteronomy 32:4).

"There is none holy as the Lord: for there is none beside thee: neither is there any rock like our God" (1 Samuel 12:2).

"For who is God save the Lord? or who is a rock save our God?" (Psalm 18:31).

IT REFERS TO THE CONFESSION OF CHRIST AS THE ROCK

Peter has just voiced his great confession of Jesus as divine Savior: *"Thou art the Christ, the Son of the living God."* Then Jesus said unto him, *"Blessed art thou, Simon Barjona: for flesh and blood hath not revealed it unto thee, but my Father which is in heaven. And I say unto thee, that thou art Peter, and upon this rock I will build my church..."* (Matthew 16:17–18).

Many biblical scholars believe that the rock to which Jesus referred was not a person at all, but the confession Peter had just made and the faith that lay behind it. The late Dr. A. T. Robertson gives this interpretation: "What is the rock on which Christ will build His vast temple? Not on Peter alone or mainly or primarily. Peter by his confession was furnished with the illustration for the rock on which His church will rest. It is the same kind of faith that Peter had just confessed."

In verse 17, Jesus says, *"Blessed art thou, Simon Barjona."* Then in verse 19, he says, *"And I say also unto thee, that thou art Peter."* When Peter was first brought to Jesus, Jesus said to him, *"Thou art Simon the son of Jona: thou shalt be called Cephas [Aramaic for*

Peter], *which is by interpretation, a stone"* (John 1:42, addition mine). Now that prophecy had been fulfilled: Simon, the son of Jona, had become Peter the rock, the redeemed man. Jesus was saying, in essence, *"Thou art Peter, the redeemed man, and upon this foundation of redeemed manhood I will build My church."* In this view, it is the confession of faith in Jesus Christ which is the foundation of the church. This familiar verse comes to mind, in which the word "profession" is synonymous with "confession."

"Fight the good fight of faith, lay hold on eternal life, whereunto thou art also called, and hast professed a good profession before many witnesses" (1 Timothy 6:12).

Clearly Timothy had made such a confession, and Paul was encouraging him by reminding him of the stand he took when he made his commitment to follow Jesus. We still make this confession today, though we call it by many different names: making a decision for Christ, praying the Sinner's Prayer, getting saved, just to name a few.

We still make this confession today, though we call it by many different names.

Only on one other occasion did Jesus make use of the word "church." This is recorded in Matthew 18:17: *"And if he shall neglect to hear them, tell it unto the church..."* Jesus had much to say about the kingdom of God and the kingdom of heaven, but only twice did He speak of the church. If He taught His disciples about the church, we have no record of it. After His resurrection, He spoke to His disciples about the kingdom of God but said nothing about the church. "To whom [the disciples] also he shewed himself alive after his passion by many infallible proofs, being seen of them forty days, and speaking of the things pertaining to the kingdom of God" (Acts 1:3, addition mine).

The church institution is not mentioned in Mark, Luke, or John. In the remainder of the New Testament, it is mentioned many times. It is used nineteen times in Acts, sixty-two times in the epistles of Paul, once in Hebrews, once in James, and twenty-three times in the writings of John (the three epistles and Revelation). Although people guess at why Jesus only mentioned the church twice, it is clear that the idea of church was in His mind. It was through the church, this living organism built of living stones fitted together, that His message of love and salvation would be introduced to the entire world. While He was alive, He left directions for how to be saved through repentance and believing on Him. It was left to Paul, Peter, and John to receive divine insight into how the church should work.

THE MEANING OF THE CHURCH

The word "church" is never used in the New Testament to refer to a house of worship; that concept was developed later. The early Christians did not have church buildings; they met in public buildings and in private homes. There is no evidence in the New Testament of a worldwide organization called "the church," such as the Roman Catholic Church. Neither is there any evidence of a national church, such as the Church of England. There is no scriptural authority for calling a group of churches of the same faith and order a church, such as the Episcopal Church, the Methodist Church, the Pentecostal Church, or the Unification Church.

What does the Bible refer to when it refers to the church? Simply put, believers are the church. Jesus is our Head and we are His body. *The body of Christ is the church.* When we speak of church we speak of those who are participants in the body of Christ.

Scripture uses several different applications when it uses this word. Some people point to Acts 9:31 as an example of the use of the word "church" to include all believers in a given territory: *"So the church throughout all Judaea and Galilee and Samaria had peace..."* (ASV). This was written in the early days of the church at a time in which we have no evidence that there were any established churches except the church in Jerusalem. In Acts 8:1 we read, *"And at that time there was a great persecution against the church which was at Jerusalem; and they were all scattered abroad throughout the regions of Judaea and Samaria..."* This speaks of the church that had rest after the conversion of Saul because he was no longer persecuting them. Years later, Paul spoke of *"the churches of Judaea"* (Galatians 1:22). The *King James Version* translates Acts 9:31 as *"Then had the churches rest,"* but the Revised Standard Version has the correct rendering: *"So the church throughout all Judea and Galilee and Samaria had peace and was built up; and walking in the fear of the Lord and in the comfort of the Holy Spirit it was multiplied"* (Acts 9:31 RSV). In this verse, Paul refers to churches of a specific region.

In a vast majority of the cases in which "church" occurs in the New Testament, the reference is to the local congregation. We find this use of the word ninety-three times. Sometimes the reference is to a particular church, as *"the church at Corinth."* And sometimes it refers to any church, as in the words of Jesus previously cited: *"Tell it to the church."*

Other expositors contend that the word "church" is always used in the New Testament in a local sense, referring to the church in either of two ways: either as an institution or in the context of His glorious return (i.e., the rapture). The two passages in which the reference is to the church in glory are Ephesians 5:27: *"That he might present it to himself a glorious church..."* and Hebrews 12:23: *"To the general assembly and church of the firstborn, which are written in heaven..."*

Thirteen passages in the New Testament use the word "church" in what some have called a figurative, or general, sense. These passages are Matthew 16:18; Ephesians 1:22, 3:10 and 21, 5:23–25, 27, 29, and 32; Colossians 1:18 and 24; and Hebrews 12:23. There are widely divergent views about these passages.

Some students of the Bible think that in most of these passages, the word "church" is used in a general sense to include all believers in the world. One consensus is that all Christians are conceived of as an ideal congregation or assembly, and that the entire community of the redeemed is an organism held together by belief in a common Lord, as well as participation in a common life and salvation, and with common aims and interests. In this picture, the church is a universal family that belongs to God. (However in light of the increase of humanism in our culture, it is important to note that although we are one in the Lord, we are each separate too. We are not part of some sort of cosmic oneness like Eastern religions preach. In Christ, we each maintain our individual and unique identities, but are still one with Him at the same time.) Some believe that the reference in these passages is to all believers of all time, both in heaven and on earth.

> The church is a universal family that belongs to God.

While there have been warm debates on these different interpretations, no vital doctrine is involved. Because Christ gave no definite teaching about the church, we may assume that He used the word in its accepted meaning in His day—as an assembly. Whether He thought of His church as including all believers everywhere will be a debatable question until the end of time when He answers it.

Interestingly the only descriptive words about the church that are found in the New Testament are "glorious" and "holy." Ephesians 5:26,27 says Jesus did all He did, *"that he might sanctify and cleanse it (the church) with the washing of water by the word, that he might present it to himself a glorious church, not having spot, or wrinkle, or any such thing; but that it should be holy and without blemish."* No other words are ever used to describe His church. Nor is the expression "the Christian church" found. Jesus sees the church as His glorious and holy bride which He bought back for Himself. This picture is also prefigured in the Old Testament in which God calls Himself the husband of His people, often using the language of this marriage relationship to reach His people: *"For thy Maker is thine husband; the Lord of hosts is his name; and thy Redeemer the Holy One of Israel; the God of the whole earth shall he be called"* (Isaiah 54:5). When Jesus secured believers to Himself through His death and resurrection power, His aim was to create a beautiful bride for Himself, one which He had made clean by His Word. To Him, we are glorious and holy. It is difficult for us to grasp this, but the New Testament clearly speaks of the church as a transformed group of people, washed *"by the water of the Word."* It also speaks of the church corporately *and* individually.

There is no other kind of church except a Christian church. This concept is important for us to consider. From God's perspective, there is only one church. In our day of thousands of groups who all

11

call themselves "churches," it is wise for us to stop and gain God's point of view. Regardless of our differences, there is only one church. Regardless of our locations worldwide, there is only one church. Free or under persecution, all races, all peoples who believe in Jesus Christ as Lord and call out to Him in faith make up one church.

Whatever the true interpretation of these different passages may be, all Bible students agree that "church" is used ninety-six times in the New Testament in which the reference plainly refers to the local congregation. Many believe the visible church of Christ is a congregation of baptized believers that are associated by covenant in the faith and fellowship of the gospel. They believe this covenanted group chooses together to observe the ordinances of Christ, be governed by His laws, and exercise the gifts, rights, and privileges invested in them by the Word of God. This group's only scriptural officers are bishops, or pastors, and deacons whose qualifications, claims, and duties are clearly outlined in the epistles to Timothy and Titus. The church needs to be in line with the Word of God and submitted to the lordship of Jesus Christ.

> **When we build a tall building, we must dig a deep foundation.**

What about Christian groups that have departed from the New Testament standard? Are they to be called churches? Some would answer in the negative, but it is perhaps better to say that they are churches that are out of order. May the Lord direct them again and bring order and peace to those groups.

When we build a tall building, we must dig a deep foundation.

No one has ever dug a deeper foundation than Jesus Christ. He did it to secure an entire family (the church) of which we all are a part. Wow! No one has ever had such a future as the bride of Christ has waiting for her.

THE CHURCH AND THE KINGDOM

The "kingdom of God" and "the kingdom of heaven" are the same. There are some who endeavor to make a distinction between them, but they are used interchangeably in the Gospels. Matthew uses the term "kingdom of heaven," while Mark and Luke use "kingdom of God." It is not wise to major on the minors and build a teaching that is not in accordance with the way Scripture uses these words. To do that will most certainly lead to doctrinal error.

Jesus mentioned the "kingdom" 112 times but spoke of the church only twice. He described the nature of the kingdom and told men how to get into the kingdom. He called it "My kingdom," just as He spoke of the church as "My church." Jesus answered, "My kingdom is not of this world..." (John 18:36). We would do well to remember this. It is not our job to build empires for Jesus. His kingdom is not of this world and He is the only one who knows how to build it properly. We're supposed to follow the dictates of the Master Builder.

Kingdom, which is *basileia*[2] in Greek, means "rule" or "reign." The kingdom of God is the rule or reign of God. It does not refer to land or territory, nor does it indicate organization. Jesus told Pilate that He had a kingdom. He told him, *"My kingdom is not of this world: if my kingdom were of this world, then would my servants fight, that I should not be delivered to the Jews: but now is my kingdom not from hence"* (John 18:36). The kingdom is not an

---

2 "Strongs's #932: basileia - Greek/Hebrew Definitions - Bible Tools," Strongs's #932: basileia - Greek/Hebrew Definitions - Bible Tools, accessed January 04, 2017, http://www.bibletools.org/index.cfm/fuseaction/Lexicon.show/ID/G932/basileia.htm.

outward one, something we can see. *"And when he was demanded of the Pharisees, when the kingdom of God should come, he answered them and said, 'The kingdom of God cometh not with observation; neither shall they say, Lo, here! or, lo, there! for behold, the kingdom of God is within you* [or in the midst of you]" (Luke 17:20–21, addition mine).

The church and the kingdom are not identical, but they work together. The church is the divine agency for promoting and extending the kingdom. The church does the business of the kingdom; the two work in tandem. Recently there has been some preaching that infers that the church is holding back the goals of the kingdom. That could never be. The true church of God will always execute the mandates of His kingdom. His kingdom springs from within all those on whom He has poured out His Holy Spirit. As the great King of Kings, He is quite competent to raise up His children in His church body and extend the borders of His kingdom at the same time.

STUDY QUESTIONS FOR CHAPTER ONE:
OUR BEGINNINGS: "UPON THIS ROCK!"

A special note: Every chapter ends with study questions. It may not be possible to use each one, so choose the questions that interest you the most for your study group time.

1. Discuss the practicality behind the choice of the word ecclesia? How did Jesus build on this Greek concept? What greater depth did He bring to the idea?

2. How many recorded times did Jesus use the word "church"? How many recorded times did Paul use the word "church"? Discuss the implications of this in your group.

3. The church is the bride of Christ. What two words does Scripture use to describe this bride? _____ and

    _____

4. Read the parable of the wedding feast in Matthew 22:1-14 together. What action does Christ expect of His people to prepare for this banquet?

5. Discuss all the different ways the word "church" has been interpreted. As a group discuss what you understand the church to be.

6. Jesus prayed that we would be one as He and His Father are one in John 17. What do you think He meant by this?

7. How does the idea that Jesus' kingdom is *not of this world* affect our decisions and our focus in life?

Chapter 2

Our Growth

The New Testament does not outline a complete, chronological picture of early church history. It's not a history book. Many churches were established in Palestine throughout the Roman Empire before the close of the first century, but only a few of them are named in the New Testament. The churches did not have distinctive names in those days either like they do today, but were named by the city or place in which they were located—for example, the church at Antioch, the church at Corinth, and the church at Rome. Paul speaks of *"the churches of Galatia"* (Galatians 1:2) and the *"churches of Asia"* (1 Corinthians 16:9). Several times he makes mention of "all churches," implying that there was a large number of them.

We are also not told how the churches were organized. There is no evidence of any definite procedure for establishing churches as we have now. The gospel was preached in communities. Men and women shared their beliefs and voluntarily banded together, following the pattern of other churches. The preacher or evangelist usually took the lead in establishing a congregation of believers in the community where he preached and won converts. Paul established a church in practically every city he visited. Then he put elders in charge of them when he left.

For a time, new churches seemed to look to the church at Jerusalem for guidance. This was probably because the Jerusalem church was the mother church and because the apostles lived there. When Philip went down to Samaria and preached about Jesus to the people, many of them believed and were baptized. The apostles at Jerusalem heard about it and immediately sent Peter and John to investigate (Acts 8:14). A company of disciples also went from Cyrene and Cyprus to Antioch and preached to the Greeks, and a great number of them believed and turned to the Lord.

> **There were no perfect churches because there were no perfect men and women.**

"Then tidings of these things came unto the ears of the church which was in Jerusalem: and they sent forth Barnabas, that he should go as far as Antioch" (Acts 11:22). Later, when trouble arose in the Antioch church over the question of circumcision, it was the Jerusalem church to which they turned for guidance.

A study of some of the representative churches reveals the fact that they were far from perfect. They were made up of men and women with all the frailties of human flesh. There were no perfect churches because there were no perfect men and women. And just as some people were better than others, some churches were better than other churches. The same is true today. The following brief look at six of the New Testament churches shows their virtues and faults.

THE CHURCH AT JERUSALEM

This was not only the first church to be established, but for some time, it was the only church. It existed for nearly ten years before the church at Antioch was organized. Because it existed on its own for a time, we know more about the church at Jerusalem than any of the others.

Their Membership

At first, the Jerusalem church was entirely Jewish, composed of Palestinian Jews, Jews from the regions beyond Judea, and Jewish proselytes. The fact that God intended to include the Gentiles as coheirs in the gospel was a hard lesson for the Jerusalem church to learn, and a matter of much debate. Although Peter opened the door of the church to the Gentiles, as revealed in Acts 10, it was Paul who became the apostle to the Gentile world. Even after Peter's experience with Cornelius, the members of the church at Jerusalem, scattered abroad by persecution, continued to preach the gospel only to the Jews (Acts 11:19).

Their Growth

Under the leadership of the apostles, they experienced rapid growth. The 120 who met in the upper room following the ascension of Christ increased to more than three thousand on the day of Pentecost, when the Holy Spirit came upon them. In the days that followed, the number grew to more than five thousand, and probably more (Acts 4:4). After that, we have no record of the number added to the church. Acts 5:14 says, "And believers were the more added to the Lord, multitudes both of men and women." The gospel was a powerful message and especially appealing to those that were oppressed: women, children, and the poor. Jesus breathed life into what had become a dead religion, and His people were ready for change.

Their Organization

The organization was very simple. With the apostles as leaders, the people came together for fellowship and worship, *"and they continued steadfastly in the apostles' doctrine and fellowship, and in breaking of bread, and in prayers"* (Acts 2:42). They had community of goods: *"And the multitude of them that believed were of one heart and of one soul: neither said any of them that ought of the things which he possessed was his own; but they had all things common"* (Acts 4:32).

This arrangement, however, was not compulsory. No one was forced to sell their possessions and put the proceeds into the common fund. When Ananias practiced deception in the matter, Peter said to him, *"Whiles it remained, was it not thine own? And after it was sold, was it not in thine own power? ..."* (Acts 5:4). The community of goods was evidently a temporary expedient and soon passed away. Only the Jerusalem church seems to have practiced it as it is not mentioned elsewhere.

Their Leadership

In the early years of its history, the church was under the direct leadership of the apostles. For a while, Peter was the principal figure. He took the lead in shaping the policies of the church, and was the chief speaker on public occasions. He led the church to accept the truth that the Gentiles were to share in the gospel privileges (Acts 11:18). But when Peter went forth on his evangelistic tours, the leadership in the church passed to James, the Lord's brother.

Internal Troubles

All was not peachy and harmonious in the church. The first breach came with the sin of Ananias and Sapphira, his wife. They sold a possession and took part of the proceeds to the common fund, pretending it was the full price they had received. They were struck dead, thus manifesting God's hatred of hypocrisy and His desire that His church should be pure.

The next trouble arose with the Greek or Hellenist believers. The Hellenists were Jews who had adopted Greek customs. They claimed that their widows were not receiving fair treatment in the distribution of the daily food. This led to the creation of the office of deacons (Acts 6:1). It is also an indicator that the church was grappling with cultural prejudice. The deacons chosen included representatives from both groups, thereby ensuring even treatment of the whole.

Persecution

From the beginning, the Jerusalem believers suffered bitter persecution at the hands of the Jews. At first, it was confined to the leaders. Peter and John were beaten and imprisoned. Stephen, one of the first deacons, was stoned to death. James, the brother of John, was beheaded. Under the leadership of Saul of Tarsus, persecution became widespread:

"As for Saul, he made havoc of the church, entering into every house, and haling men and women committed them to prison" (Acts 8:3).

Under the heavy hand of persecution, the church was scattered abroad. However, great good came from it: *"Therefore they that* were scattered abroad went every where preaching the Word" (Acts 8:4).

This led to the spread of the gospel and the establishment of other churches throughout Palestine and beyond. In AD 70, a Roman army under Titus captured and destroyed Jerusalem. Fearing this catastrophe and the suffering it would bring, the Christians of Jerusalem left the city shortly before its capture and fled to Pella, in Perea. They remained there until it was safe to return to Jerusalem, but the church in Jerusalem never regained its former prestige.

THE CHURCH AT ANTIOCH

This is the second church about which we have any definite information. The story of its beginning is found in Acts 11. A group of men from Cyrene and Cyprus, driven by the hand of persecution, went to Antioch and preached to the Greeks. Great numbers believed and turned to the Lord. The church at Jerusalem sent Barnabas to investigate the work. This good man saw that a real work of grace was going on, and he did all within his power to encourage the brethren: *"Who, when he came, and had seen the grace of God, was glad, and exhorted them all, that with purpose of heart they would cleave unto the Lord"* (Acts 11:23).

> **Barnabas, feeling the need for help, went to Tarsus and enlisted Saul, who was now called Paul.**

The work grew, and Barnabas, feeling the need for help, went to Tarsus and enlisted Saul, who was now called Paul. Under the ministry of these two men, the church continued to grow in numbers and influence. It was at Antioch that the disciples were first called "Christians" (Acts 11:26). It was not long before the church at Antioch surpassed the church at Jerusalem in leadership and influence. What were the things that made it great? Let's look at three specific characteristics.

It Was Thoroughly Evangelized

The church at Antioch refused to be held under bondage to Jewish legalism. The membership of the church consisted of both Jews and Gentiles; this gave rise to controversy. Certain men came down from Jerusalem and insisted that the Gentile Christians must submit to the rite of circumcision or they could not be saved (Acts 15:1). A delegation was sent to the church at Jerusalem to get counsel on this vital matter. The result was a complete vindication of those who contended that salvation was by grace through faith and did not depend on anything else. No physical proof of salvation was necessary; man need do nothing to add to the work God had already done in a person's heart. So the church was freed from the chains of Judaism and assumed its place of leadership in the Christian world. It is in this decision that the Christian church first became distinct.

It Was a Missionary Church

When Saul of Tarsus was converted, the Lord told him he was chosen to deliver the gospel to the Gentile world: *"But rise, and stand upon thy feet: for I have appeared unto thee for this purpose, to make thee a minister and a witness both of these things which thou hast seen, and of those things in the which I will appear unto* thee; delivering thee from the people, and from the Gentiles, unto whom now I send thee" (Acts 26:16–17).

The time had now come for Saul to start on that work. As the leaders in the church at Antioch began doing service for the Lord, the Holy Spirit said to them, *"Separate me Barnabas and Saul for the work whereunto I have called them"* (Acts 13:2). There was immediate obedience to this divine command: *"And when they had fasted and prayed, and laid their hands on them, they sent them away"* (Acts 13:3). The great missionary enterprise to carry the gospel all over the Roman Empire was launched.

It Was a Benevolent Church

The church at Antioch shared willingly and gladly with those who were in need. When tidings reached them that there was suffering among the brethren at Jerusalem, they sent aid at once: *"Then the disciples, every man according to his ability, determined to send relief unto the brethren which dwelt in Judaea: which also they did, and sent it to the elders by the hands of Barnabas and Saul"* (Acts 11:29–30).

THE CHURCH AT PHILIPPI

Paul and Silas established this church on Paul's second missionary journey. It was the first church organized on European soil. Acts 16 tells us that it started with a band of women who met by a river for prayer: *"And on the sabbath we went out of the city by a river side, where prayer was wont to be made; and we sat down, and spake unto the women which resorted thither"* (Acts 16:13). Years later, when Paul was writing from a Roman prison to this church, he spoke of "those women who labored with me in the Gospel" (Philippians 4:3). It was in this city that Paul and Silas were beaten and cast into prison, but they turned their suffering into glorious victory for Christ and left a flourishing church. This church was noted especially for two things.

Its Liberality

The church at Philippi was one of the most liberal of all the churches. It gave of its means for the support of Paul in his missionary work. *"Now ye Philippians know also, that in the beginning of the gospel, when I departed from Macedonia, no church communicated with me as concerning giving and receiving, but ye only. For even in Thessalonica ye sent once and again unto my necessity"* (Philippians 4:15–16).

When Paul was in prison at Rome, the Philippian church sent gifts to him more than once: *"But I rejoiced in the Lord greatly, that now at the last you're care of me hath flourished again..." "But I have all, and abound: I am full, having received of Epaphroditus the things which were sent from you"* (Philippians 4:10, 18).

The church also made liberal contributions to the collection Paul was taking for the poor saints at Jerusalem: *"Moreover, brethren, we do you to wit of the grace of God bestowed on the churches of Macedonia, how that in a great trial of affliction the abundance of their joy and their deep poverty abounded unto the riches of their liberality. For to their power, I bear record, yea, and beyond*

> The church at Philippi was one of the most liberal of all the churches.

their power they were willing of themselves; praying us with much intreaty that we would receive the gift..." (2 Corinthians 8:1–4).

Its Joy

Paul spoke of *"the abundance of their joy."* It was a joy that triumphed over affliction and trials: *"In a great trial of affliction the abundance of their joy and their deep poverty abounded unto the riches of their liberality"* (2 Corinthians 8:2).

Paul seems to have gotten more joy and satisfaction from the church at Philippi than from any of the many churches he established. His epistle to the church has a note of joy running all the way through it. He uses the word "rejoice" eight times. His feeling toward the church is best expressed in these words: *"Therefore, my brethren dearly beloved and longed for, my joy and crown..."* (Philippians 4:1).

THE CHURCH AT THESSALONICA

Leaving Philippi, Paul and his companions went to Thessalonica, where they soon won a band of disciples and established a church. In this church were *"devout Greeks a great multitude, and of the chief women not a few"* (Acts 17:4).

Their Zeal

Paul commended the church at Thessalonica for its possession of the three great Christian graces: faith, hope, and love: *"Remembering without ceasing your work of faith, and labor of love, and patience of hope in our Lord Jesus Christ"* (1 Thessalonians 1:3).

This church was also noted for its evangelistic and missionary zeal: *"For from you sounded out the word of the Lord not only in*

Macedonia and Achaia, but also in every place your faith to God-ward is spread abroad; so that we need not to speak any thing" (1 Thessalonians 1:8).

Confusion in Thessalonica

One thing caused confusion in the church. Many of the members thought the coming of the Lord was at hand, so they felt no need to work anymore. They were spending their time in idleness, waiting for the Lord to come. Paul wrote his second epistle to the church to set them straight on this important truth. He assured them that the Lord would certainly come, but the time of His coming was not for man to determine. Their business was to do the work the Lord had given them to do: "Therefore, brethren, stand fast, and hold the traditions which ye have been taught, whether by word, or our epistle" (2 Thessalonians 2:15).

THE CHURCH AT CORINTH

This is another of the churches founded by Paul on his second missionary journey. There he met two notable Christians who became his close friends and helpers: Aquila and his wife, Priscilla.

Problems in Corinth

Located in one of the wickedest cities in the world, it is not surprising that the church at Corinth had many issues with which to contend. It was torn by factions: *"For ye are yet carnal: for whereas there is among you envying, and strife, and divisions, are ye not carnal and walk as men?"* (1 Corinthians 3:3). It was also beset with immorality: *"It is reported commonly that there is fornication among you, and such fornication as is not so much as named among the Gentiles, that one should have his father's wife"* (1 Corinthians 5:1).

The members were going to court, one against another: *"Now therefore there is utterly a fault among you, because ye go to law one with another"* (1 Corinthians 6:7). The church was guilty of disorderly conduct at the observance of the Lord's Supper (1 Corinthians 11). It was also disturbed over questions about eating meat that had been offered to idols (1 Corinthians 8) and the gift of tongues (1 Corinthians 14). These and other problems confronted the Corinthian Christians.

This church probably caused Paul more concern than any other. Some of the members were disposed to question his authority as an apostle, disregard his injunctions, and live as they pleased. Paul used some rather sharp language in rebuking them. He reminded them that he had *"robbed other churches, taking wages of them,"* that he might serve the church at Corinth. He condemned them for their immorality, their contentious spirit, and their worldly ways.

Paul's Exhortations and Advice

Paul called on them to *"Examine yourselves, whether ye be in the faith"* (2 Corinthians 13:5). Yet he expressed the assurance that they were real Christians: *"I rejoice therefore that I have confidence in you in all things"* (2 Corinthians 7:16). He exhorted and encouraged them constantly, saying, *"Know ye not that ye are the temple of God, and that the Spirit of God dwelleth in you?"* (1 Corinthians 3:16), and reminding them and urging them to live their lives in a worthy manner.

THE CHURCH AT ROME

We have no definite information concerning the founding of this church. We do not know who established it or when it was established. One this is certain: The Roman Catholic Church's claim that it was founded by Peter is false. There is not even a suggestion in the New Testament that Peter had anything to do with this church. There is no sure proof that he was ever in Rome.

Neither was the church at Rome founded by Paul. The church was there long before Paul ever visited Rome. It may have been founded by men and women who were converted under the ministry of Paul at other places that had later gone to Rome. Or it may have been founded by those converted under another's ministry. We do not know.

However, Paul had much to do with the development of this church. His epistle to the Romans contains the fullest discussion of the greatest Christian doctrines to be found in the New Testament. During his years of imprisonment at Rome, he was in close touch with the church there and won many more converts.

> **Rome came to hold a prominent place among the churches.**

All Roads Lead to Rome

It is not hard to understand how the church at Rome came to hold a prominent place among the churches. It was strategically located in the world's capital, and it was said that "all roads led to Rome." Visitors from every section of the empire went to Rome. Many of them were Christians and naturally went home and told others about the church in Rome.

The Roman church was a great church in many respects. Paul

29

held it in high esteem: *"I thank my God through Jesus Christ for you all, that your faith is spoken of throughout the whole world"* (Romans 1:8).

"And I myself also am persuaded of you, my brethren, that ye are full of goodness, filled with all knowledge, able also to admonish one another" (Romans 15:14). But the Roman church laid no claim to preeminence among the churches. That was a development that came about many years later.

Other Churches

There were other churches just as important as those already studied here. In the second and third chapters of Revelation are the messages of the living Christ to the seven churches of Asia: Ephesus, Smyrna, Pergamos, Thyatira, Sardis, Philadelphia, and Laodicea. In all of them except for one—Smyrna—the Lord found something to condemn; and in all, except for one—Laodicea—He found something to commend.

Some Bible scholars think the messages to these seven churches, while they deal with conditions that existed at that time, also constitute a preview of the whole church age from the first century to the end of time, culminating in the apostasy described in the message to the church at Laodicea. That may or may not be accurate, but there is certainly an appeal in these messages to the churches for all time: *"He that hath an ear, let him hear what the Spirit saith unto the churches"* (Revelation 2:11) is the refrain running through all the messages.

And Then What Happened?

Within little more than fifty years, the churches grew from one church in Jerusalem to a great host of churches scattered throughout the Roman Empire. It has been estimated that there were *over*

500,000 Christians in the world at the close of the first century. This number constitutes over 12.5% of the world's population at that time.

The churches of the New Testament suffered much persecution. At first it came from the Jewish leaders, but over time they were targeted by the Romans authorities too. In 2 Corinthians 11:24–27, Paul tells of some of the trials he suffered.

> # Roman Empire looked on the church as an illegal society.

The Jews hated the early Christians because they considered them apostates to the faith of their fathers. They treated Christianity as "a heretical sect within Judaism"[3] that needed to be stamped out. Jewish persecution began with the beating and imprisonment of Peter and John. This was followed by the stoning of Stephen and widespread persecution under the leadership of Saul of Tarsus. After Saul's conversion, his name was changed to Paul. He, in turn, suffered at the hands of the Jews when he became a Christian and an apostle of Jesus Christ, and eventually went on to stand before the emperor of Rome for his faith. He was jailed often and a portion of his letters to the church are called "prison epistles" because they were written while he was under arrest.

Over time, the Roman Empire looked on the church as an illegal society and treated Christians as nonbelievers because they would not embrace the religion of the empire and worship Caesar. Roman persecution began with the desire of Roman officials to win the favor

---

3 Justo L. González, The story of Christianity, Peabody, MA: Prince Press, 1999, 32.

of the Jews, but as the Christian religion spread over the Roman Empire, it drew the attention of the authorities for other reasons. By the second century, there were widespread rumors throughout the empire that Christians were cannibals and believed in incest. These claims sound fantastic today, but at the time, were serious threats. They were both misunderstandings of Christian practices: one of Communion in which believers "ate and drank" the body and blood of Christ, and the other of Christian gatherings, called "love feasts,"

In spite of persecution, the faith of the Christians continued to spread.

to which only the baptized were admitted. Since Christians commonly called each other by the terms "brother" and "sister," it was believed they had orgies at these closed events.[4] As a result of these and other mistaken perceptions of the Christian faith, Christians were beaten, imprisoned, and stoned. Some were burned at the stake, some were thrown to wild beasts and torn to bits, and others were crucified. But, in spite of persecution, the faith of the Christians continued to spread. The men and women of the early church era had tremendous conviction and courage. They were bound together by their common faith and were ready to die for it.

Finally in AD 311 and AD 313, two edicts were set forth which brought an end to Christian persecution in the Roman Empire. Emperor Galerius became convinced that his disease was the punishment of God for the killing of Christians. Interestingly in his

---

4 Ibid. 49,50.

proclamation, he asked that Christians would pray to their god for public leaders to bring peace to the state.[5] This was followed soon after his death by the Edict of Milan in AD 313 through Emperor Constantine. Eventually every soldier would be required by the state to go to church.[6]

The church was about to make some big changes. Once the government sanctioned the church, many practices that were associated with respect for the emperor slowly crept into the church. These included the use of incense, genuflecting (bowing), and robes for the clergy. Choirs followed and over time, a separation between laity and clergy arose. More and more church buildings were established: many on the graves of the martyrs. Superstitious ideas about the bones of the martyrs gave rise to almost magical beliefs in relics. Although preachers in the church did not hold with these ideas, the church was growing too fast to check them.[7]

Over time, the Roman church would emerge historically as the leading church, primarily because the Roman state now espoused the religion and gave power to its leaders. This was to have disastrous effects on the purity of the church so that by the end of a thousand years, a great division would bring forth the first two denominations: the Roman Catholic Church and the Eastern Orthodox Church. Due to corruption in the church, poor doctrine, and its mistaken hold in politics, there would be yet another even more dramatic splintering five hundred years later when the Reformation brought forth the Lutherans, the Swiss Protestants, the Anabaptists, the Baptists, and many other denominations, plunging Europe into a series of religious wars for years and years. Around the same time, King Henry VIII took this occasion to break away from Rome too, and founded the

5 Ibid. 106.

6 Ibid. 123

7 Ibid. 125.

Church of England with himself as the head.

Since that time, the Christian church has broken into more and more denominations. Today we are scattered over a thousand hills. Thankfully the Lord knows how to lead the church through His Holy Spirit and although we will never be one denomination on the earth again, we will be one with Jesus in the end.

STUDY QUESTIONS FOR CHAPTER 2:
OUR GROWTH

1. When Paul and the early apostles began a church, how did they go about it?

2. Where was the first church founded, and what were some of its attributes?

3. In what area was the term "Christian" first coined?

4. Review the messages to the churches found in Revelation 3. What can we glean from each of these messages?

5. Do you think we live in a Laodicean age? Or do you think that message is ageless? Discuss this point and its repercussions in the church.

6. What were the effects of persecution on the church?

7. Some persecution came because of ignorance of Christian practices in the early church age. Many believers perished because of it. How is our culture today increasingly ignorant of Christian beliefs? Is there any way this situation can be rectified?

8. The gospel claims that salvation is through Christ alone and requires a surrender of our will to His, thus it will always be an unpopular message in the world. Discuss the balancing act between standing for the truth of the gospel without compromise and "living at peace with all men" (Romans 12:18).

9. How did imperial interference slowly dilute and corrupt the message of the church?

10. Today the body of Christ is largely denominational, but even non-denominational churches develop a flavor of their own.

Every group has its own merit and unique focus, and it's when every believer is put together that we have the entire body of Christ. Discuss what the many Christian groups (Baptists, Catholics, Pentecostals, Mennonites, etc.) bring to the table.

Chapter 3

Our DNA

It would be wise to begin this section with the reminder that the church is not a building and the word "church" is never used in the New Testament to designate a building. It was several centuries after the apostolic age before this unfortunate use of the word began. In the New Testament, the word "church" always refers to people—redeemed people and baptized believers who are voluntarily associated with the worship and service of God. Because it is the one institution left on earth by the Lord to carry on His work, it is important for us to understand something about its nature, its DNA.

THE CHURCH IS A DIVINE INSTITUTION

Eight times in the New Testament, the church is called *"the church of God."* Paul speaks of *"the churches of God"* (1 Thessalonians 2:14) and *"the churches of Christ"* (Romans 16:16). There are four basic ways in which the church is a divine institution.

A Divine Architect Planned It

The idea of the church did not originate in the mind of man, but in the heart of God. When God was ready to establish His tabernacle, He called Moses up to the mountain and gave him a definite plan for the structure, setting forth the dimensions, the materials to use in constructing it, and its furnishings. He warned Moses: *"See, saith he, that thou make all things according to the pattern shewed to thee in the mount"* (Hebrews 8:5).

> The idea of the church did not originate in the mind of man, but in the heart of God.

When God was ready to establish the church, which was to be the temple of the Holy Spirit, He specified the pattern by which it was to be fashioned; this pattern is described in the New Testament. And God still warns men today, *"See that ye make it according to the pattern showed you in the Book."* God's plan is never out of date. The style of church architecture has changed throughout the centuries, but God's plan for His church has not changed. The blueprint for this century is the same as it was for the first century. The original plan is still available. Different church plans have come and gone, but the only abiding plan is His plan.

A Divine Builder Constructed It

Jesus said, *"Upon this rock I will build my church."* Christ is the Builder of the church. It is not a church unless Christ builds it. Concerning the first church in Jerusalem, the Bible says, *"And the*

Lord added to them day by day those that were saved" (Acts 2:47 ASV). The Lord chooses and shapes the material that goes into the construction of His church. There is no place in the church for men and women whom the Lord has not added. We often speak of a certain number of additions to the church. Let us be sure the Lord has added them.

A Divine Purchaser Bought It

Paul speaks of *"the church of God, which he hath purchased with his own blood"* (Acts 20:28). Again he says, *"As Christ also loved the church and gave himself for it"* (Ephesians 5:25). He reminded the Corinthians that they were not their own but were bought with a price (1 Corinthians 6:19–20). The church belongs to God because He purchased it at a great price. He has never relinquished His claim. Men have been entrusted with the administration of the affairs of the church, but it does not belong to them. Scripture tells us that *"without the shedding of blood there is no forgiveness of sins"* (Hebrews 9:22 RSV); it is the core of our connection with God. We must never stray away from this truth.

The Divine Lord Has Commissioned It

Jesus said to the band that made up the nucleus of the first church, *"As my father hath sent me, even so send I you"* (John 20:21). A little later, He said to a larger group, *"Go ye therefore, and teach all nations, baptizing them in the name of the Father, and of the Son, and of the Holy Ghost: teaching them to observe all the things whatsoever I have commanded you"* (Matthew 28:19–20). The church is the one institution the Lord established on earth through which to carry out His program, His Great Commission. We have a great inheritance which we are to pass on to the next generation, and this rejoinder to share our faith is not just for the preacher, but for every Christian. Every one of us is commissioned by God to bear fruit that abides.

THE CHURCH IS A SPIRITUAL ORGANISM

The church is more than an organization; it is an organism. An organism is something that has life. A machine is an organization made up of many parts, but it is not an organism. It has no life. In His message to the church at Sardis, the Lord said, *"I know thy works, that thou hast a name that thou livest, and art dead"* (Revelation 3:1). It had ceased to be an organism and had become a mere organization. The church is spiritual.

> **He calls us His children.**

There is a reason God uses terms for living things to describe His people. He calls us His children. God Himself is our Father. He says we are sheep and need a Shepherd (John 10). He says we are trees and that we bear fruit. He tells us there are two kinds of fruit: the fruit of the flesh and the fruit of the Spirit (Galatians 5:19-23). He tells us we are branches in His vine and He will prune us so we will increase as fruit-bearers (John 15). Only living things are born, reproduce, and grow; God uses all these pictures to describe His church and the individuals that comprise it.

Spiritual Experience and Spiritual Life

The body of Christ is composed of those who have had a spiritual experience and who possess a spiritual life. No one is a fit subject for membership in the church until he or she has been born again. There is no evidence that anyone ever became a member of a New Testament church until that person experienced the new birth that comes through faith in the Lord Jesus Christ. In every case, either by direct statement or necessary implication, members of the New Testament churches are represented as believers in Christ. This is important because just as the chromosomes in DNA produce a child with the characteristics of its mother and father, so the Lord produces fruit through His Holy Spirit that is like Him. Without His divine nature within us, we are not His children and are helpless to effect change in ourselves or anyone else. As Scripture says:

"But to all who received him, who believed in his name, he gave power to become children of God; who were born, not of blood nor of the will of the flesh nor of the will of man, but of God" (John 1:12,13 RSV).

We are God's *"workmanship, created in Christ Jesus for good works, which God prepared beforehand, that we should walk in them"* (Ephesians 2:10). That is saying that we are like His poetry to the world: His living, breathing message of love. We must be born through Him and walking in a spiritual life to accomplish this.

It Is the Dwelling Place of the Spirit of God

In writing to the church at Corinth, Paul said, *"Know ye not that ye are the temple of God, and that the Spirit of God dwelleth in you?"* (1 Corinthians 3:16). Because the church is the temple of God, it is to be kept pure and clean: *"If any man defies the temple of God, him shall God destroy; for the temple of God is holy, which temple you are"* (1 Corinthians 3:17).

On two occasions, Jesus cleansed the temple in Jerusalem, overturning the tables of the money changers and driving out those who bought and sold. In like manner, He would drive out of the church, His spiritual temple, all who defied Him. Each of us is individually a temple of God.

41

THE CHURCH IS A BLOOD-BOUGHT GROUP OF PEOPLE

Let us turn again to Paul's exhortation to the elders of the church at Ephesus: *"Take heed therefore unto yourselves, and to all the flock, over which the Holy Spirit has made you overseers, to feed the church of God, which he has purchased with his own blood"* (Acts 20:28).

These words bear eloquent testimony to the deity of Jesus Christ. Most of the revisers have changed the passage to read *"the church of the Lord,"* but the two oldest manuscripts of the Scriptures have it just as it appears in the King James Version, *"the church of God."* There was deity in the sacrifice of Calvary. Mere human blood could never redeem men from sin. Removing our sin required the blood of a perfect sacrifice, a sinless one, a sacrifice that could only be made through the One who never sinned, yet had the opportunity to do so. Thus, God allowed His deity to rest in mankind so He could buy back His dearest creature: you and me.

The church is a blood-bought church. Any organization or institution that is not based on that fundamental truth is no church of God and has no right to call itself a church. Satan's masterpiece in the realm of institutions is a hypocritical church, one that pretends to be a church of God but is not. Instead it is a social club. The mark of a genuine Christian is a blood mark, and the mark of a genuine church is a blood mark. *It is the blood of Jesus that powerfully changes us and makes us different from the cold institutions the enemy raises up.* They are not the same.

The church is made up of individuals, and if the church is to be a blood-bought church, the individuals who make up the church must be, and admit that they are, blood-bought individuals. There is no place in the church of God for unsaved men and women. They must be clothed in garments that have been washed completely and thoroughly in the blood of the Lamb. They must be unashamed to call Jesus Christ their Lord.

In that striking parable of the Great Supper, Jesus told of a king who made a marriage feast for his son. The guests were invited, and the hall was filled. When the king entered the hall to greet his guests, he saw a man who did not have on a wedding garment. He said to him, "Friend, how camest thou hither not having a wedding garment?" The man was speechless (Matthew 22:12).

There is no place in the church of God for unsaved men and women.

When our Lord comes into His church and finds those in His membership who have not been redeemed in His blood, He will ask that same searching question: "How came ye in hither not having wedding garments, garments washed and made clean and white in the cleansing blood of the Lamb?" This parable ends with the familiar statement that *many are called but few are chosen,* meaning that many are invited to the feast, called to know God, but few actually heed that call and respond in the way He has outlined. There has never been a time when we needed to emphasize the necessity of a blood-bought membership in the church of God more than now.

THE CHURCH IS A DEMOCRATIC ORGANIZATION

The churches of the New Testament were established on

democratic principles. Each church was a self-governing body, and the members enjoyed equality of privileges. There were no super-organizations to dictate and no overlords to rule. This subject is discussed more fully in the chapter on church government.

Something of the nature of the church is set forth in the symbols that are used to describe it. Three deserve special consideration.

A Building

Christ thought of His church as a spiritual building. He said, *"Upon this rock I will build my church."* Several other passages of Scripture refer to the church as a building as well.

> ## Christ thought of His church as a spiritual building.

In 1 Corinthians 3, Paul said to the church, *"Ye are God's building"* (verse 9) and *"Know ye not that ye are the temple of God?"* (verse 16). In 2 Corinthians 6:16, He calls the church a temple: *"For ye are the temple of the living God; as God hath said, I will dwell in them, and walk in them; and I will be their God, and they shall be my people."*

The word *naos*[8] is translated as "temple" in these passages. It means "sanctuary" and includes the Most Holy Place where God promised that His presence would abide. *This means that the church is the Holy of Holies in which the Spirit of God dwells.* This means that the Holy One dwells in every Spirit-filled blood-bought believer.

---

8   "Strongs's #3485: naos - Greek/Hebrew Definitions - Bible Tools," Strongs's #3485: naos - Greek/Hebrew Definitions - Bible Tools, accessed January 05, 2017, http://www.bibletools.org/index.cfm/fuseaction/Lexicon.show/ID/G3485/naos.htm.

In Ephesians 2:20–22, we find this description of the church: *"And are built upon the foundation of the apostles and prophets, Jesus Christ himself being the chief cornerstone; in whom all the building fitly framed together growth unto an holy temple in the Lord: in whom ye also are builded together for an habitation of God through the Spirit."* In this passage, as in the preceding one, the church is described as a holy temple for the habitation of God.

Third, Peter makes use of the same figure in Peter 2:5: *"ye also, as lively stones, are built up a spiritual house, and holy priesthood, to offer up spiritual sacrifices, acceptable to God by Jesus Christ."* The church is a spiritual temple, in which all believers are priests unto God, and they are to offer spiritual sacrifices to God.

The Bible speaks of three sacrifices that are to be offered to God.

1. The sacrifice of a broken spirit — *"The sacrifices of God are a broken spirit: a broken and contrite heart, O God, thou wilt not despise"* (Psalm 51:17). God sometimes despised the sacrifices the people took to the altar because they were blemished, but He never despised the sacrifice of a broken spirit and a contrite heart because it is evidence of humility. God always receives a humble heart.

2. The sacrifice of praise — *"By him therefore let us offer the sacrifice of praise to God continually, that is, the fruit of our lips that give thanks to his name"* (Hebrews 13:15). That is another sacrifice that always pleases God. It does not depend on how a person feels. The sacrifice of praise speaks of praising God in every circumstance, no matter what.

3. The sacrifice of dedicated lives — *"I beseech you therefore, brethren, by the mercies of God, that ye present your bodies a living sacrifice, holy, acceptable unto God, which is your* *reasonable* [spiritual] *service"* (Romans 12:1, addition mine). This is the evidence of a life that is responding to God daily.

When we live lives that are devoted to God, these sacrifices will be present in our lives. They are hallmarks of true faith and an authentic Christian walk. Only an authentic Christian walk will produce them.

A Body

Several times in the New Testament, the church is described as being the body of which Christ is the head: "And hath put all things under his feet, and gave him to be the head over all things to the church. Which is his body, the fullness of him that filleth all in all" (Ephesians 1:22–23).

"And he is the head of the body, the church" (Colossians 1:18).

"For as we have many members in one body, and all members have not the same office: So we, being many, are one body in Christ, and every one members one of another" (Romans 12:4–5).

The longest passage in which the church is described as a body is 1 Corinthians 12:12–27. In these verses, Paul tells how the body is made up of many members, differing in size and function, but each doing its part and all working together. In like manner, the church is made up of many members, differing in talent and place, but each is to do his or her part, and all are to work together without schism under the direction of Christ, the Head of the church. This synergy in the church is what makes it work. Paul writes also to beware of particular problems that can break down this unity of the body: comparing ourselves to one another (2 Corinthians 10:12), allowing bitterness to take root in our hearts (Hebrews 12:15), and much else. It is important to maintain a healthy body individually and corporately.

In both of these symbols, the church as a building and the church as a body, two truths are emphasized: diversity and unity. The building is made up of many stones, differing in shape and size, but they all fit together, each one in its place, and they make one building. The body is made up of many members, each in its place and with its own function, all working together as one body. So in the church, there is diversity and unity—many living stones, but one spiritual house; many individual members, but one body.

A Bride

This symbol is brought over from the Old Testament. Hosea the prophet represents God as saying to His people in Israel, *"And I will betroth thee unto me forever; yea, I well betroth thee unto me in righteousness, and in judgment, and in lovingkindness, and in mercies. I will even betroth thee unto me in faithfulness: and thou shalt know the Lord"* (Hosea 2:19–20).

Isaiah used the same symbol to set forth the vital relationship between God and His people: *"For thy Maker is thine husband, the Lord of hosts is his name"* (Isaiah 54:5).

Forsaking the Lord for idols was considered spiritual adultery: *"The Lord said also unto me in the days of Josiah the king, hast thou seen that which backsliding Israel hath done? She is gone upon every high mountain and under every green tree, and there hath played the harlot"* (Jeremiah 3:6).

"Turn, O backsliding children [Israel], saith the Lord; for I am married unto you" (Jeremiah 3:14, addition mine).

"Surely as a wife treacherously departeth from her husband, so have ye dealt treacherously with me, O house of Israel, saith the

Lord" (Jeremiah 3:20).

In the New Testament, we find the church represented as the bride of Christ: *"Wherefore, my brethren, ye also are become dead to the law by the body of Christ; that ye should be married to another, even to him who is raised form the dead, that we should bring forth fruit unto God"* (Romans 7:4).

"For I am jealous over you with godly jealousy: for I have espoused you to one husband, that I may present you as a chaste virgin to Christ" (2 Corinthians 11:2).

> # In the New Testament, we find the church represented as the bride of Christ.

The figure of the church as the bride of Christ refers more specifically to the glorified church. The classic passage on this is found in Ephesians 5:25–32: *"Husbands, love your wives, even as Christ also loved the church, and gave himself for it; that he might sanctify and cleanse it with the washing of water by the word, that he might present it to himself a glorious church, not having spot, or wrinkle, or any such thing; but that it should be holy and without blemish. So ought men to love their wives as their own bodies. He that loveth his wife loveth himself. For no man ever yet hated his own flesh; but nourisheth and cherisheth it, even as the Lord the church: For we are members of his body, of his flesh, and of his bones. For this cause shall a man leave his father and mother, and shall be joined unto his wife, and they two shall be one flesh. This is a great mystery: but I speak concerning Christ and the church."*

The spiritual marriage between Christ and His church will be consummated when He comes in glory and gathers His people unto Himself: *"Let us be glad and rejoice, and give honor to him: for the marriage of the Lamb is come, and his wife hath made herself ready. And to her was granted that she should be arrayed in fine linen, clean and white; for the fine linen is the righteousness of saints. And he saith unto me, Write, Blessed are they which are called unto the marriage supper of the Lamb"* (Revelation 19:7–9).

In all three of these symbols of the church—a building, a body, and a bride—the truth of the close and vital relationship between Christ and His church stands out. Each one emphasizes a particular truth concerning that relationship.

In the symbol of a building, the idea of strength and security prevails. The church is built on a sure foundation. It is built on a rock, and storms cannot destroy it. *"The gates of hell [Hades] shall not prevail against it"* (Matthew 16:18, addition mine).

The church, likened to a body, suggests service. The members of a body are the instruments through which work is accomplished, all responding to the directions that go out from the head. The head says to the hand, "Move," and it moves. It says to the foot, "Go," and it goes. It is through the church, His body, that Christ does His work in the world. Each member has his or her own place to fill and work to do, under the direction of Christ, the Head.

The figure of the bride suggests purity: *"For I have espoused you to one husband that I may present you as a chaste virgin to Christ"* (2 Corinthians 11:2).

"That he might sanctify and cleanse it with the washing of water by the word, that he might present it to himself a glorious church, not having spot, or wrinkle, or any such thing; but that it should be holy

and without blemish" (Ephesians 5:26–27). The church as the bride of Christ must be pure.

There are other figures that symbolize the relationship between Christ and His church in which the church is not definitely mentioned. One of these is found in John 15:5: *"I am the vine, ye are the branches."*

The central truth emphasized here is that of fruit bearing: *"He that abideth in me, and I in him, the same bringeth forth much fruit"* (John 15:5).

"Herein is my Father glorified, that ye bear much fruit" (John 15:8).

Another symbol is the shepherd and the flock: *"I am the good shepherd: the good shepherd giveth his life for the sheep"* (John 10:11).

This symbol stresses the thought of divine care and the believer's security: "My sheep hear my voice, and I know them, and they follow me; and I give unto them eternal life; and they never perish, neither shall any man pluck them out of my hand. My Father, which gave them me, is greater than all; and no man is able to pluck them out of my Father's hand" (John 10:27–29).

In these passages, the relationship between Christ and the individual believer is especially stressed, but the larger relationship is implied. There are many branches, but one vine. There are many sheep, but one flock and only one Shepherd.

One cannot study the nature of the church without being impressed with the fact that church membership is not to be taken lightly. It calls for clean living and consecrated service. No real Christian wants to be a crumbling stone in a spiritual house, or a diseased member in the body of Christ. Neither does anyone wish to be a stain on the bride of Christ, a fruitless branch on the vine, or a straying sheep in the flock. It is our goal to be fitted stones, healthy members of the body, that are clean, connected, and close to the Savior of our souls.

STUDY QUESTIONS FOR CHAPTER THREE: OUR DNA

1. The word "church" always refers to a _____ of _____. This may seem obvious, but people today often think of the building first when they think of church. Why is this reminder important? What truths will we miss if we don't understand this?

2. What is the significance of God as the divine Architect of His church?

3. What is the significance of God as the divine Builder of His church?

4. How has God commissioned His people? What does He expect of us?

5. Using the ideas behind natural birth, consider why it is important that believers are born properly into the kingdom? As leaders what problems have you seen with those who have not been born and raised properly?

6. We were "bought with a price." A song we sing says that we will never understand how much it cost God to send His Son to redeem us. In Genesis, God prevented Abraham from doing the very thing He was going to do: sacrificing His own son. Consider your own children and discuss what this sacrifice reveals about the Father's heart.

7. The Bible compares the church to a building, a body, and a bride. Consider the function of each. How do these pictures help us understand different facets of our relationship with our Father?

8. How should the knowledge that we are the church affect the way we live our lives?

Chapter 4

Church Government

God did not leave the governing of His body to chance. Jesus did not birth the church, and say, "Go ahead. Do it anyway you please." Just as Scripture holds the blueprint for how the church should be built, it also gives direction for how the church should be run. This chapter will go over that direction, but before we do, let's look at the four basic forms of church government that have grown up in the world today.

Autocratic — The best example of an autocratic church is the Roman Catholic Church. In the Roman Catholic Church, the pope, who is considered infallible by members, stands at the head of a worldwide organization. Under him is a graded ministry. The local congregation has little voice in the affairs of the church, and people attend the church that is in their region. They are told what they are to believe and what they are to do. Complete obedience is required.

Episcopal — This name is derived from the Greek word episcopos, which means bishop, or overseer. The Episcopal and

Methodist churches are the major representatives of this system. The college or board of bishops makes up the "superior clergy," and under them stand the "inferior clergy." The highest authority is vested in the bishops.

Presbyterian — As indicated by the name, this form of church government is represented by the Presbyterian Church. The name is derived from the Greek word presbyteros, meaning a presbyter, or elder. Two classes of elders are recognized – teaching elders and ruling elders. The church session is composed of the churches in a given district. Higher in authority than the Presbytery is the Synod, and the highest authority of all is vested in the General Assembly.

Congregational—According to this form, each church is an independent, self-governing body. There is no super-organization with authority to legislate for the churches. Each congregation manages its own affairs without interference from any other body. Within this non-denominational form though, some church governments can still become autocratic, in that the one man, usually called the pastor, rules everything and what he says, goes. Others of this type function under the governing of a plurality of elders with pastors, teachers, evangelists, prophets, and apostles all working together under the lordship of Christ.

Which of these forms of church government most nearly approximates that of the New Testament churches? Some advocates of these various forms of church government do not claim scriptural authority for their particular systems. They do not deny the authority of the Scriptures, but their contention is that the New Testament does not reveal a definite form of government for the churches. Therefore, it is left to the churches to work out the system that best suits their needs. The Catholic Church, of course, claims equal authority with the Scriptures. It holds that only the germ of church government is revealed in the

Scriptures and that it was left to the church to develop a complete system, hence Catholics hold church tradition on an equal or greater footing as Scripture itself. We who are of the Pentecostal persuasion, along with others, believe that the norm of church government is clearly set forth in the New Testament. We believe that the blueprint in the Scripture trumps human tradition and organization.

Organization in the New Testament churches seems to have had a gradual development under the leadership of the apostles and the Holy Spirit, or under the leadership of the Holy Spirit through the apostles. The first church at Jerusalem started with a very simple organization. It was composed of a company of men and women meeting together, with the apostles as leaders. With the growth and spread of Christianity, and the organization of new churches, church organization assumed a definite form. There were two outstanding characteristics.

IT WAS A DEMOCRATIC ORGANIZATION

The word "democracy" comes from two Greek words that mean "rule of the people." A democratic form of government is that in which supreme authority rests in the people. In this sense, the New Testament churches were democratic organizations. Let's look at three aspects of democratic organizations.

Voluntary Membership

No one became a member of the church by birth. The fact that a child had parents who were godly church members did not open the door of the church to them. Neither was one coerced into church membership, nor compelled to remain a member against his or her wishes. Jesus never used coercion. He said, *"Behold, I stand at the door, and knock: if any man hear my voice, and open the door, I* will come in to him, and will sup with him, and he with me" (Revelation 3:20). He did not force His way in. The door had to be opened voluntarily. Jesus' lament over Jerusalem was voiced in these words: *"O Jerusalem, Jerusalem, thou that killest the prophets, and stonest them which are sent unto thee, how often would I have gathered thy children together, even as a hen gathereth her chickens under her wings, and ye would not!"* (Matthew 23:37). He wanted them to come to Him, but He did not force them. They made the choice. That means that you are not a Christian simply because you were born into a Christian family. Your commitment to Christ is your choice.

> # Your commitment to Christ is your choice.

Some of Jesus' disciples wanted to coerce men. One day John said to Jesus, *"Master, we saw one casting out devils in thy name: and we forbad him, because he followeth not with us"* (Luke 9:49). But Jesus replied, *"Forbid him not."* Some of the blackest pages in Christian history have been written by men who sought to compel others to conform to their religious beliefs. Both Catholics and Protestants have been guilty of this. Many people have erred in this way over the years, but let it be said that today we will no longer lift the hand of persecution or seek to win converts by force.

Church membership was a voluntary relationship among New Testament churches, entered into by deliberate choice. People might be influenced by others in making their decision, but the choice was their own. Coercion in religion is contrary to the principles and practices of New Testament churches. It rarely, if ever, bears the proper fruit, which is a convert that has had a born-again conversion experience and whose desire is to follow God with all their heart. This is the primary reason why Jesus appealed to the hearts of His hearers.

Equality of Privileges

In a true democracy, every member has equal rights and privileges; there are no overlords. The young and the old, the rich and the poor, the educated and the ignorant: all stand on equal footing. Some, by reason of ability and training, may become leaders, but not lords.

This was true in the early Christian churches. Jesus said to His disciples, *"Ye know that the princes of the Gentiles exercise dominion over them, and they that are great exercise authority upon them. But it shall not be so among you: but whosoever will be great among you, let him be your minister; and whosoever will be chief among you, let him be your servant"* (Matthew 20:25–27).

In Old Testament days, there were priests who ministered in the temple. They offered sacrifices and made intercession for the people. The High Priest alone had the right to enter into the Holy of Holies, where God had promised that His presence would abide. This privilege belonged to the High Priest only and he only exercised that privilege once a year. But in the New Testament churches, all believers were priests unto God, having the right to approach God for themselves: *"But ye are a chosen generation, a royal priesthood, an holy nation, a peculiar people; that ye should shew forth the praises of him who hath called you out of darkness into his marvelous light"* (1 Peter 2:9).

"Unto him that loved us, and washed us from our sins in his own blood, And hath made us kings and priests unto God and his Father" (Revelation 1:5–6).

The believer needs no official aid in his or her approach to God, and no person on earth, whether priest or potentate, has any right to stand between a soul and God.

Self-Government

The New Testament church was a self-governing body. There were rulers in the Jewish synagogues, but there were no rulers in the churches. The apostles, who occupied a unique place in early Christianity and had no successors, made no effort to dictate to the churches. When trouble arose in the church at Jerusalem over the distribution of the common funds, the apostles did not appoint men to look after these matters. Instead, they called on the whole congregation to elect them (Acts 6:3).

Peter, the recognized leader and spokesman for the Twelve, did not exalt himself above the others but referred to himself as a fellow elder: *"The elders which are among you I exhort, who am also an elder"* (1 Peter 5:1).

He did not command; he exhorted. He spoke of the commandments to the churches as coming from the Lord through the apostles: *"That ye may be mindful of the words which were spoken before by the holy prophets, and of the commandment of us the apostles of the Lord and Savior"* (2 Peter 3:2).

Paul, the greatest of all apostles and the one who organized more churches than anyone else, did not try to manage the affairs of the churches either. When he spoke or wrote by inspiration, he gave it as the command of the Lord, not his own: *"And unto the married I command yet not I, but the Lord, let not the wife depart from her husband"* (1 Corinthians 7:10).

"Now concerning virgins I have no commandment of the Lord;

yet I give my judgment, as one that hath obtained mercy of the Lord to be faithful" (1 Corinthians 7:25).

"If any man think himself to be a prophet, or spiritual, let him acknowledge that the things that I write unto you are the commandments of the Lord" (1 Corinthians 14:37). When there was need for discipline in the Corinthian Church, Paul called on the church to exercise that discipline: *"Therefore put away from among yourselves that wicked person"* (1 Corinthians 5:13).

It was the responsibility of each congregation of believers to govern themselves wisely and according to the Word of God. Although we have a hierarchy in our churches today, each believer still has the responsibility of being his brother's keep so that the body of Christ functions properly.

THE CHURCHES WERE INDEPENDENT ORGANIZATIONS

Each New Testament church was an independent unit. The churches welcomed advice from others, but recognized no authority except that of Christ. Let's look at two important ways in which these churches were independent.

Independent in Their Relationships with Other Churches

One church did not interfere in the affairs of another church, and certainly no church had the right to dictate to another church. If any church could have laid claim to any such right, it would have been the church at Jerusalem. It was the first church, and for some time it was the only church. In a sense, it was the mother church. Naturally it would have a deep interest in other churches and was ever-ready to extend a helping hand, but its people made no effort to tell the others what to do.

It is true that certain individuals in the church did try to control the policies of other churches. Some of them went to Antioch and insisted that the Gentile converts to the Christian faith would have to submit to the Jewish rite of circumcision, or they could not be saved: *"And certain men which came down from Judaea taught the brethren, and said, Except ye be circumcised after the manner of Moses, ye cannot be saved"* (Acts 15:1).

The brethren at Antioch sent Barnabas and Paul to discuss the matter with the church at Jerusalem. The result was a repudiation of the troublemakers and a friendly letter of advice to the church at Antioch *"with Paul and Barnabas; namely, Judas surnamed Barnabas, and Silas, chief men among the brethren"* (Acts 15:22). The friendly and courteous letter the church at Jerusalem sent is recorded in Acts 15:22–29. It contains no note of authority but exhorts the Gentile Christians to abstain from certain practices that would give offense to their Jewish brethren. Never does it dictate terms to the Antioch Church. Instead it is an appeal, nothing more.

In New Testament Christianity, there was no super-organization seeking to impose its will on the individual churches. There was no law-making body that issued regulations to the churches. The leadership might receive aid from other churches, but they were in no manner subject to them.

This is a principle that our Pentecostal churches need to guard with zealous care. *Centralization of authority has no place among Pentecostal or any other denominational churches.* Associations and conventions may plan and advise, but they may not dictate or regulate. Boards and committees are set up—not to tell the churches what they must do but to carry out the expressed will of the churches.

The churches do not need super-bodies to hand down decrees. The Holy Spirit that dwells in the churches is the all-sufficient Guide to every church.

While the churches of the New Testament were independent in their relations with each other, there was a spirit of cooperation among them. They worked together toward a common cause. An example of cooperation is found in the collection taken for the poor saints at Jerusalem. Paul called on all the churches to participate in this work of charity, and they made a willing and ready response. They were able to do this without surrendering any of their individual sovereignty.

> # Cooperation is the secret of success among the churches.

Cooperation is the secret of success among the churches. Certain phases of the work are too vast for any one church to accomplish alone. By pooling their resources and working together, the best results are obtained. There could be no great missionary or benevolent enterprise without cooperation among the churches.

Independent in Their Relationships with Civil Government

Our Lord stated the principle by which Christians are to be guided when He said, *"Render therefore unto Caesar the things which are Caesar's; and unto God the things that are God's"* (Matthew 22:21).

We usually refer to this as the relationship between church and state. According to the First Amendment to the US Constitution, adopted in 1791, the two are to operate in different spheres—the church in the field of religion and the state in the field of government.

The two are to be kept separate and distinct. The state is not to interfere in the affairs of the church, and the church is not to interfere in the affairs of the state. Yet the two are to live and work in a friendly and mutually helpful relationship.

The Christian is a citizen of two countries—the kingdom of God and the one he or she currently lives in. The good Christian will be a good citizen of both, rendering to his or her country the things that belong to it and rendering to God the things that belong to God. Let's look at three responsibilities that Christians must exercise toward the government.

Obedience

This expectation was enjoined by both Peter and Paul. Peter gave this advice to the Christians, to whom he wrote, *"Submit yourselves to every ordinance of man for the Lord's sake: whether it be to the king, as supreme; or unto governors, as unto them that are sent by him for the punishment of evildoers, and for the praise of them that do well. For so is the will of God, that with well doing ye may put to silence the ignorance of foolish men: as free, and not using your liberty for a cloke of maliciousness, but as the servants of God. Honor all men. Love the brotherhood. Fear God. Honor the King"* (1 Peter 2:13–17).

To the Roman church, which was under the shadow of Caesar's throne, Paul wrote, *"Let every soul be subject unto the higher powers. For there is no power but of God: the powers that be are ordained of God. Whosoever therefore resisteth the power, resisteth the ordinance of God: and they that resist shall receive to themselves damnation [condemnation]. For rulers are not a terror to good works, but to the evil. Wilt thou then not be afraid of the power? Do that which is good, and thou shalt have praise of the same: for he is the minister*

*of God to thee for good. But if thou do that which is evil, be afraid…
for he is the minister of God, a revenger to execute wrath upon him
that doeth evil"* (Romans 13:1–4).

Financial support

As good citizens, they pay their taxes. It was the question of
tribute that called forth the just cited statement from Jesus: *"Render
therefore unto Caesar the things which are Caesar's; and unto God
the things that are God's."* The Pharisees and Herodians had asked
Jesus *"Is it lawful to give tribute unto Caesar, or not?"* (Matthew
22:17). In Romans 13:6–7, Paul says, *"For this cause pay ye tribute
also: for they are God's ministers, attending continually upon this
very thing. Render therefore to all their dues: tribute to whom tribute
is due; custom to whom custom; fear to whom fear; honor to whom
honor."*

Participation

Christians have no right to criticize unless they are doing their
part to make their government what it ought to be. They can do this
by exercising their right to vote, giving moral support to those whose
duty it is to make and enforce the laws, and helping to mold public
opinion and maintain a healthy moral atmosphere.

There are duties that a Christian owes to God, and these are
supreme. When there is conflict between the laws of man and the
laws of God, the Christian must obey God. That is the principle that
Peter voiced when he stood before the Sanhedrin: *"And when they
had brought them, they set them before the council: and the high
priest asked them, saying, Did not we straitly command you that ye
should not teach in this name? And, behold, ye have filled Jerusalem
with your doctrine, and intend to bring this man's blood upon us.
Then Peter and the other apostles answered and said, "We ought to*

obey God rather than men" (Acts 5:27–29).

Certainly there was no sign of union between church and state in the early days of the church. The churches did not meddle in the affairs of the government and they denied the right of the government to interfere with them as well. While Christians were persecuted by the government in the days of the apostles—violating a sacred principle—it was not until the fourth century that a definite union between church and state was consummated. This took place when Constantine, the Roman emperor, embraced Christianity. In the centuries that followed, sometimes that state was in the ascendancy, controlling the church, and sometimes the church was supreme, dictating to the state. But during that period, small Christian groups refused to submit to the decrees of either church or state and were persecuted by both.

It is here, in the relationship between church and state that a grave danger is arising today: the danger of blending God's laws with man's laws in the church. There is a growing tendency on the part of certain religious organizations to bring the church and state into partnership. This is true especially in the field of education.

The union of church and state has always been attended by many evils. It has resulted in the loss of religious freedom, a formal church without spiritual power, and constant bickering and strife. Some of our church fathers led in the fight for religious liberty in this land and won a glorious victory. It cost them blood and tears, but they did not hesitate to pay the price. They were beaten, imprisoned, and insulted, but they refused to give up. And it was this group who had a large share in writing the First Amendment to the Constitution, granting religious liberty to all. The fruit of their victory must not be allowed to perish through the indifference of their children.

STUDY QUESTIONS FOR CHAPTER FOUR: CHURCH GOVERNMENT

1. Of the four types of church government outlined in the beginning of this chapter, which one do you think best reflects the plan for the church in the New Testament?

2. Why is it important that following Jesus be a free will choice?

3. The Old Testament made promises that mankind would at some future time have God's Spirit dwelling within: Emmanuel, God with us. Discuss how this has changed the way men relate to God.

4. How should we be our brother's keeper today?

5. "In New Testament Christianity, there was no super-organization seeking to impose its will on the individual churches. There was no law-making body that issued regulations to the churches. The leadership might receive aid from other churches, but they were in no manner subject to them." Discuss this point as a group. Why is the ability of each congregation to rule itself so vital to the health of the body? What responsibility does it entail?

6. It was when the Roman state first got involved in the affairs of the church that policies began to go awry. Historically, this bears out. In every instance where the state and the church try to unite and dictate their will on the population, it is a disaster. Why does this not work? Interestingly there have been multiple attempts to do this in the guise of unity. Why is this attempt always outside God's will?

7. How should we be properly related to our governments according to the Word of God?

Chapter 5

Our Leaders

As we have seen, the early church developed gradually. If Jesus gave His disciples any specific direction concerning these matters, we have no record of it. In the first church at Jerusalem, the apostles were recognized as the leaders. The organization was rather simple. There seems to have been no definite officers except the apostles. With the growth of the church, under the guidance of the Holy Spirit, new leaders were named. However, not a great deal is revealed in the New Testament about these leaders; and much that has been revealed has been the subject of controversy.

There are two passages in which various officers are listed. In 1 Corinthians 12:28, we have one list given by Paul: *"And God hath set some in the church, first apostles, secondarily prophets, thirdly teachers, after that miracles, then gifts of healings, helps, governments, diversities of tongues."*

Paul writes a similar list in Ephesians 4:11: *"And he gave some, apostles; and some, prophets; and some, evangelists; and some, pastors and teachers."* Most of these seem to refer to special callings bestowed on individuals rather than offices in the church. These people are God's gifts to the church.

The word "apostle" comes from a Greek word that means "send." Apostles were men sent forth on a special mission. It was the name Jesus gave to the twelve men whom He chose to be with Him and whom He trained to carry on His work after His departure: *"And when it was day, he called unto him his disciples: and of them he chose twelve, whom also he named apostles"* (Luke 6:13).

> The apostles were not church officers, but they exercised a general ministry.

Following the death of Judas, the church at Jerusalem chose Matthias to fill the vacancy. Nothing further is known of his life, so some think that his election, which took place before the coming of the Holy Spirit, may have been of men and not of God. Later, Paul became an apostle by appointment of the Risen Lord: *"Paul, a servant of Jesus Christ, called to be an apostle"* (Romans 1:1).

The first qualification of an apostle seems to have been that he had seen the Lord. Paul based his right to be called an apostle on that fact: *"Am I not an apostle? Am I not free? Have I not seen Jesus Christ our Lord?"* (1 Corinthians 9:1).

The apostles were not church officers, but they exercised a general ministry—first under Jesus Christ and then under the Holy Spirit. The early apostles had no successors.

Neither were the prophets considered church officers. The name indicates a special gift. They were men chosen of God to receive and impart God's messages to men. There is no evidence that the church ever elected anyone to the prophetic office. They were prophets by appointment of God in the New Testament just as they were in the Old Testament.

The same is true of the others Paul mentioned, such as evangelists, teachers, and those who had been given power to work miracles, heal the sick, and speak in tongues. None of these designated a definite office in the church, but referred to men endowed of God for special service. Paul confirmed this: *"Having then gifts differing according to the grace that is given to us, whether prophecy, let us prophesy according to the proportion of faith; Or ministry, let us wait on our ministering: or he that teacheth, on teaching"* (Romans 12:6–7).

"For to one is given by the Spirit the word of wisdom; to another the word of knowledge by the same Spirit; to another faith by the same Spirit; to another the gifts of healing by the same Spirit; to another the working of miracles; to another prophecy, to another discerning of spirits; to another diverse kinds of tongues; to another the interpretation of tongues; but all these worketh that one and selfsame Spirit, dividing to every man severally as he will" (1 Corinthians 12:8-11). The same man might be endowed with several of these gifts. Although these gifts we not ordered by men, they were received and recognized by the early church, and they still are today. God's callings in these areas cannot be hidden. As such, when they become evident in a person, they should be recognized and encouraged.

As the church developed, two offices became definite and permanent: those of elder and deacon. Let's take a look at the details surrounding these two prominent church positions.

THE ELDER

The elder was also called bishop and pastor. These three names are synonymous terms for the same officer.

"Elder," as the name indicates, originally referred to an older man. But it came to be used in an official sense to designate those with experience and who were worthy of respect. The literal meaning of "bishop" is overseer, one who exercises oversight in the church. "Pastor" means shepherd, one who is to feed and care for the flock. Each of these words focuses on specific jobs within the body, but they can all be done by one person.

The fact that these three names refer to the same office is evident when we examine two passages of Scripture in which the three names occur or are inferred. The first is Acts 20:17: *"And from Miletus he sent to Ephesus, and called the elders of the church."* Speaking to the same group in verse 28, Paul says, *"Take heed therefore unto yourselves, and to all the flock, over which the Holy Ghost hath made you overseers* [bishops], *to feed* [act as shepherd or pastor] *the church of God"* (additions mine). Thus, the same officers are spoken of as elders, bishops, and pastors.

The second passage is 1 Peter 5:1–2: *"The elders which are among you I exhort, who am also an elder, and a witness of the sufferings of Christ, and also a partaker of the glory that shall be revealed; Feed* [pastor] *the flock of God which is among you, taking the oversight* [bishop] *thereof"* (additions mine). Paul refers to himself as an elder and exhorts the other elders to "pastor" their congregations. The word "bishop" was added here to refer to pastors who had oversight of more than one flock. The point is that many words were used to describe the function of this office in the body of Christ. They were responsible to lead the flock of God. They were in charge of feeding them, which refers to the preaching and teaching of His Word. Just as Jesus is our Shepherd, they were to act in a similar fashion: protecting the people of God from bad doctrine and the assaults of the enemy. They did this through prayer, study, teaching, and loving conversation. Their lives were fueled by the compassion of their Savior, and exemplified their own personal relationships with Christ.

The names "elder" and "bishop" are found many times in the New Testament, but that of "pastor" occurs but once in the our English translation, in Ephesians 4:11. Is it not a little curious that the word we use most often to describe the leader in the church is the one the New Testament used least? You hardly ever hear of a pastor referred to as an elder. It almost sounds irreverent, but which one is more biblically correct? Actually "elder" is. Over time, the word "pastor" supplanted that of "elder" culturally. It may have grown out of the unscriptural associations that became connected with the terms "elder" and "bishop" through historical abuse of that office. Some of our forefathers, recoiling from this, reverted to "pastor" as a term that had not been spoiled but still signified what it was intended to mean in the New Testament writing. Even though the terminology has changed, the fivefold ministry gift functions today as it ever did. Whether we call them

> **Many words were used to describe the function of this office in the body of Christ.**

71

pastors, bishops, or elders does not matter that much. God gave them as a gift to His church so it could be loved and maintained in health. Under their leadership, the body of Christ is edified and built up. These leaders are under-shepherds who must, in their turn, submit to the one true Shepherd: Jesus Christ. When this is in order, the body grows and becomes strong.

Let's look even more closely at what the New Testament says about the pastor. Let's examine the six specific aspects Scripture outlines about the role of these leaders who are so vital to the health and growth of the body of Christ.

A Plurality of Pastors

There seems to have been a plurality of pastors in the New Testament churches. Four times in Acts 15, Luke refers to *"the apostles and elders"* in the church at Jerusalem (verses 2, 4, 6, 23). Concerning the churches that Paul and Barnabas established on their first missionary journey, Acts 14:23 says, *"And when they had ordained them elders in every church, and had prayed with fasting, they commended them to the Lord in whom they had believed."*

Paul called for the elders of the church at Ephesus (Acts 20:17). James said, *"Is any sick among you? Let him call for the elders of the church..."* (James 5:14). Every time the term is mentioned in connection with the churches, it is always plural, not singular. Just how many elders a church had, or whether different churches had different numbers, we are not told.

There is a growing trend today to return to this idea in the church. More and more we hear of churches with multiple pastors. Many times they will have a lead pastor, a teaching pastor, a youth pastor, a discipleship pastor, an evangelist, even an executive pastor. These distinctions allow the man or woman of God who is called as a pastor to focus on their particular bent and work together as a team at the same time.

Ordination

The pastors, or elders, are spoken of as having been ordained: *"And when they had ordained elders in every church"* (Acts 14:23).

In his epistle to Titus, Paul said, *"For this cause left I thee in Crete, that thou shouldest set in order the things that are wanting, and ordain elders in every city, as I had appointed thee"* (Titus 1:5).

Nothing definite, however, is given as to the method of ordination. A suggestion is given in the account of setting apart of Paul and Barnabas for missionary service by the church at Antioch: *"And when they [the prophets and teachers in the church] had fasted and prayed, and laid their hands on them, they sent them away"* (Acts 13:3).

It would seem that a service such as this was used in setting the pastor apart for this work. Paul exhorted young Timothy, *"Neglect not the gift that is in thee, which was given thee by prophecy, with the laying on of hands of the presbytery"* (1 Timothy 4:14). This does not mean that the gift was bestowed by the laying on of the hands of the presbytery, but that the bestowal of the gift was accompanied by the laying on of hands led by the Holy Spirit. The calling to be a pastor comes from God, and is recognized by the body. A teacher cannot help but teach. A pastor will naturally do the work of a pastor, and so on.

Those who are already ordained and chosen by God have the authority to then lay hands on that person to bless them and agree with the gift God has put in them, but it is a spiritually given gift. The gift is given by God alone, and should be. A true bishop does not have that position because they chose it. They must be chosen by God and the gift must be initiated by the Holy Spirit according to God's will. This is the proper process for ordination.

Election

The manner of electing pastors is not clearly stated in the New Testament. Paul and Barnabas were set apart for missionary service by the church at Antioch at the direction of the Holy Spirit (Acts 13:2). These two missionaries ordained elders in the churches they established (Acts 14:23). Paul instructed Titus to *"ordain elders in every church"* (Titus 1:5). The inference is that these elders were first chosen by the church.

There is no word in the New Testament about the tenure of office of the elders. It would seem that they were not elected for any definite time. Neither is there any information concerning the call of an elder from one church to another, or what procedure was followed if an elder moved from one church to another.

Qualifications

The qualifications for a pastor or elder were of a high order. There are two passages of Scripture in which these qualifications are clearly stated. In both of these passages, he is called "bishop." *"This is a true saying, if a man desire the office of a bishop, he desireth a good work. A bishop then must be blameless, the husband of one wife, vigilant, sober, of good behavior, given to hospitality, apt to teach; not given to wine, no striker, not greedy of filthy lucre; but patient, not a brawler, not covetous; one that ruleth well his own house, having his children in subjection with all gravity; (for if a man know not how to rule his own house, how shall he take care of the church of God?) not a novice, lest being lifted up with pride he fall into the condemnation of the devil. Moreover he must have a good*

74

report of them which are without; lest he fall into reproach and the share of the devil" (1 Timothy 3:1–7).

"If any be blameless, the husband of one wife, having faithful children not accused of riot or unruly. For a bishop must be blameless, as the steward of God; not selfwilled, not soon angry, not given to wine, no striker, not given to filthy lucre; but a lover of hospitality, a lover of good men, sober, just, holy, temperate; holding fast the faithful word as he hath been taught, that he may be able by sound doctrine both to exhort and to convince the gainsayers" (Titus 1:6–9).

The qualifications set forth in these two passages are very similar. Paul makes it plain that one who aspires to be a pastor must have an untarnished reputation and an upright character. In addition, he must be able to teach. In short, he must be a man endowed by nature, grace, and training. It is evident that Paul believed in a trained ministry.

No true minister will claim that he has fully measured up to the high ideal set forth by Paul.

No true minister will claim that he has fully measured up to the high ideal set forth by Paul, yet no true minister would ever wish to lower that standard. Satisfaction with low standards of character or conduct is a barrier to the ministry, as is satisfaction of a substandard understanding of God's Word. And satisfaction with one's attainments, either spiritual or mental, will clip the wings of any person's ministry as well. It is far better for pastors to remain ever dependent on the Holy Spirit, growing in grace and humility.

Duties

The duties of the pastor, or elder, are clearly defined in the New Testament. It is implied in the name "bishop" that he was to exercise oversight in the church. The name "pastor" or "shepherd" indicated that he was to feed and care for the flock. He was a preacher, teacher, leader, and counselor. He was a sympathetic friend and a faithful servant of the church. His job was a big responsibility. As such, he was to receive respect and honor from the church: *"And we beseech you, brethren, to know them which labor among you, and are over you in the Lord, and admonish you; And to esteem them very highly in love for their work's sake..."* (1 Thessalonians 5:12–13).

"Let the elders that rule well be counted worthy of double honor, especially they who labor in the word and doctrine" (1 Timothy 5:17).

Today we would do well to return to a healthy respect for the office of pastor. Unless one has spent a lot of time with a pastor, it is hard to imagine what they deal with regularly. Their lives aren't just about standing in a place of honor, preaching the Word, and being continually blessed. They take on the burden of their people: counseling, comforting, praying, discipling, teaching, preaching, and modeling a life devoted to Jesus Christ. Many pastors are on call continually. And they are accomplishing this while working and raising their own families at the same time. This is the reason that it is imperative that the men and women who get ordained as pastors really are called by God to the position.

Support

More than once, Paul declared that those who labor in the gospel are to receive support from those among whom they minister. In writing to the Corinthian church, he said, *"Do yet not know that they which minister about holy things live of the things of the temple? And they which wait at the altar are partakers with the altar? Even so hath the Lord ordained that they which preach the gospel should live of the gospel"* (1 Corinthians 9:13-14). In Old Testament times, the priests who ministered in the temple received adequate support. Paul indicated that the same should be true in the New Testament churches.

But the pastor, or elder, was not to be a money lover. One of the qualifications of a bishop was that he was not to be *"greedy of filthy lucre."* Much of the time, Paul made a living for himself by the work of his hands, rather than to appear to be preaching for money. To the elders of the church at Ephesus, he said, *"I have coveted no man's silver, or gold, or apparel. Yea, ye yourselves know, that these hands have ministered unto my necessities, and to them that were with me"* (Acts 20:33–34).

> Today we would do well to return to a healthy respect for the office of pastor.

There is no evidence that a stipulated amount the pastor was to receive was agreed on. However, there is nothing that would forbid this either. The principle is laid down: *"The laborer is worthy of his hire"* (Luke 10:7). Certainly, the arrangement should be to remove from the pastor's mind all cause for worry over financial support, but it is a sad day in any church when the pastor comes to think more of salary than he does of souls.

No verse in the New Testament holds up the work of the pastor as an easy job. Paul spoke of it as labor: *"Let the elders that rule well be counted worth of double honor, especially they who labor in the word and doctrine"* (1 Timothy 5:17). The word "labor," as translated, means "toil." The man who is looking for easy work has no place in pastoral ministry. It may be one of the most stressful and difficult jobs ever. However, for the pastor who stays connected and humble, it is the culmination of a life called to fulfill the ministry of God Himself. A high calling indeed, and not one to be dismissed because of difficulty. When God calls, God equips.

THE DEACON

The word "deacon" is a translation of the Greek word *diakonos*[9] which means "servant," referring either to accomplishing servile work or as an attendant rendering free service. It is used in the New Testament in both an official and unofficial way. Sometimes it is used to refer to those who minister in the home: *"His mother saith unto the servants* [deacons], *Whatsoever he saith unto you, do it"* (John 2:5, addition mine).

It also refers to civil rulers: *"For he is the minister [deacon] of God to thee for good…"* (Romans 13:4, addition mine).

Paul spoke of himself as a minister (deacon): *"Who then is Paul, and who is Apollos, but ministers* [deacons] *by whom ye believed…"* (1 Corinthians 3:5, addition mine).

Jesus was called a deacon: *"Now I say that Jesus Christ was a minister* [deacon] *of the circumcision for the truth of God, to confirm the promises made unto the fathers"* (Romans 15:8). In the literal

---

9 "Strongs's #1249: diakonos - Greek/Hebrew Definitions - Bible Tools," Strongs's #1249: diakonos - Greek/Hebrew Definitions - Bible Tools, accessed January 04, 2017, http://www.bibletools.org/index.cfm/fuseaction/Lexicon.show/ID/G1249/diakonos.htm.

meaning of the word, every Christian is a deacon.

But the name came to designate those who are selected for special duties in the church. On at least two occasions, Paul used the word in that manner: *"Paul and Timotheus, the servants of Jesus Christ, to all the saints in Christ Jesus which are at Philippi, with the bishops and deacons..."* (Philippians 1:1). The letter was addressed to all the members of the church (to all saints) and made special mention of those who held official positions (bishops and deacons).

Having set forth the qualifications of bishops, Paul said, *"Likewise must the deacons be grave,"* (1 Timothy 3:8). Thus, an ordinary word in common use came to have special significance. In this verse, "grave" means to have integrity and to be worthy of respect. Four aspects of this office are explored in Scripture.

Origins

It is generally agreed, though denied by some, that the office of deacon had its beginning in the controversy that arose in the church at Jerusalem over the daily administration of the common fund. The title of "deacon," however, does not appear in the account given by Luke: *"And in those days, when the number of the disciples was multiplied, there arose a murmuring of the Grecians against the Hebrews, because their widows were neglected in the daily ministration. Then the twelve called the multitude of the disciples unto them, and said, It is not reason that we should leave the word of God, and serve tables. Wherefore, brethren, look ye out among you seven men of honest report, full of the Holy Ghost and wisdom, whom we may appoint over this business. But we will give ourselves continually to prayer, and to the ministry of the word"* (Acts 6:1–4).

The apostles' suggestion met the hearty approval of the members of the church, so they chose seven men and set them before the apostles. These men were set apart, or ordained, to their office by prayer and the laying on of the apostles' hands just as elders were: *"Whom they set before the apostles; and when they had prayed, they laid their hands on them"* (Acts 6:6). There was probably no special significance in the number seven suggested by the apostles. Some have thought that because seven was considered a sacred number, and that every church should have just seven deacons, but the number should be determined by the size of the church.

It was the Greeks who started the murmuring that led to the creation of the office of deacon. The Greeks mentioned here were Jews who adopted the Greek language and customs. They were probably in the minority in the church. It is significant that all of the seven men chosen had Greek names, indicating that they were all chosen from the group that was complaining. No more complaining was heard. This was a wise way to bring an end to what might have developed into a first-class church fuss.

There are one or two passages of Scripture that have been interpreted as furnishing biblical precedent for the election of deaconesses. In Romans 16:1, Paul speaks of Phebe as *"a servant (diakonon) of the church which is at Cenchrea."* Whether Paul used the word in its general sense of servant or in an official sense is not made clear. The fact that Phebe was spoken of as a servant of the church probably indicates a special relationship.

In the midst of his discussion about the qualifications of the deacon, Paul said, *"Even so must their wives be grave, not slanderers, sober, faithful in all things"* (1 Timothy 3:11). However, "wives" is a mistranslation. The correct word is "women." Again, it is not clear whether he was referring to the wives of deacons, to women in general, or to women who held some official position in the church. The fact that Paul made this statement in the heart of his discussion of the office of deacon indicates that he made reference to either the wives of deacons or women who served as deaconesses. Either way there was clearly a place for women who qualified. **Election**

If the account in Acts 6 is to be accepted as giving the origin of the office of deacon, then the manner of electing deacons is plainly stated: *"Then the twelve called the multitude of the disciples unto them, and said, 'It is not reason that we should leave the word of God, and serve tables. Wherefore, brethren, look ye out among you seven men of honest report...'"* (Acts 6:2–3). They were not appointed by the apostles but elected by the whole church.

> There was clearly a place for women who qualified.

The manner of their ordination is also given: *"...whom they set before the apostles: and when they had prayed, they laid their hands on them"* (Acts 6:6). They were set apart by prayer and the laying on of the hands of the apostles.

Nothing is revealed in the New Testament about deacons' tenure of office. Presumably, the deacons were elected for life or for the duration of their good behavior. However, the absence of any specific information concerning this would indicate that it was not a matter of supreme importance. Much is to be said in favor of a rotating system for deacons. And it certainly is not true that because someone is suited to be a deacon in one church, they are therefore suited to be a deacon in a different church. We must be open to the direction of the Holy Spirit in this matter. Just as seasons change, so can the fitting of a person for this kind of position. Some people serve as deacons for many years and then do something else.

Qualifications

The apostles established three qualifications for the seven men chosen by the church at Jerusalem: *"of honest report,"* *"full of the Holy Ghost,"* and *"wisdom."* They were to be men of good reputation in the community, whose lives were dominated by the Holy Spirit, and of practical wisdom or common sense.

Paul described the qualifications more fully in 1 Timothy 3–10 and 12: *"Likewise must the deacons be grave, not double-tongued, not given too much wine, not greed of filthy lucre; holding the mystery of the faith in a pure conscience. And let these also first be proved; then let them use the office of deacon, being found blameless... Let the deacons be the husbands of one wife, ruling their children and their own houses well."*

The qualifications for a deacon are very similar to those a bishop should possess. It is a big responsibility and requires the same manner of commitment. The deacon must be right in character, sincere in speech, temperate in habits, liberal in giving, sound in doctrine, and exemplary in his or her family relations. It is a high standard, one to challenge the best of men or women. Many churches have suffered through the selection of unworthy men or women to serve as deacons. *Financial ability and social standing do not make one fit to be a deacon.* On the other hand, one is not to decline to serve as a deacon because he feels himself unworthy. If it were a question of worthiness, no one would be elected. The office should seek the man; the man should not seek the office.

Duties

The duties of the deacon are not clearly outlined in the New Testament. The men chosen in the church at Jerusalem were to look after the administration of the common fund. But the qualifications laid down for a deacon would indicate that he was to do more than *"serve tables."* He was to be a spiritual leader. At least two of the seven became evangelists: Steven and Philip. It was Stephen the deacon who was the first of the early Christians to seal his testimony with blood, to lay down his life in loyalty to his Lord.

Some of the duties deacons are supposed to perform are looking after the finances of the church, assisting in the administration of the ordinances, ministering to the poor, exercising a watchful care over the congregation, giving attention to discipline, and taking a leading part in all of the activities of the church.

A great reward is promised to those who serve well as deacons: *"For they that have used the office of a deacon well purchase to themselves a good degree, and great boldness in the faith which is in Christ Jesus."* (1 Timothy 3:13). This probably points to a richer experience in the Christian life and a stronger and more courageous faith in Christ Jesus.

The honest and sincere deacon will endeavor to prepare himself for the best service in his office. He will inform himself not only about the immediate duties of his office but concerning the whole program of the church and the work of the kingdom. He will make use of every opportunity to gain a wider vision and a more thorough understanding of Christian stewardship.

Someone may ask, what about the other officers, such as clerk, treasurer, and trustees? These are not unscriptural, but rather in the nature of helpers. Paul lists those whom God hath set in the church as *"helps."* No one knows for sure just what he meant by this. Certainly, it is not contrary to Scripture for the church to appoint helpers in carrying out its programs. It is only common sense that these positions would be necessary to the workings of the church.

STUDY QUESTIONS FOR CHAPTER FIVE:
OUR LEADERS

1. There is an old saying that "the ground is level at the foot of the cross." Discuss what this means and how it relates to the people and leaders of the church.

2. The church has witnessed a terminology war over the position of pastor.

3. The early church was run by a plurality of elders. Do you think that template works for the twenty-first century church? Why or why not?

4. Pastors do well to remember that they too are part of the sheepfold and under one Shepherd. What suggestions do you have for your brothers and sisters who lead the flock of God, to ensure their well-being and success?

5. How does a person's calling reveal itself in the body? Discuss this in regard to the preacher, prophet, teacher, and evangelist gifts.

6. Sometimes people become deacons in the church that are not fitted for the position. What should we look for when choosing deacons?

7. In many ways the gift of helps undergirds the work of the church. Make a list of the ways this gift is seen in the church. Make it a point to encourage and affirm those in your church with this gift.

8. Scripture tells us, *"they are not wise, measuring themselves, as they do, by one another and comparing themselves with one another"* (2 Corinthians 10:12b WNT). Discuss the pitfalls of comparison in the body of Christ.

Chapter 6

Church Ordinances

There are four Greek words that are translated "ordinances" in the King James Version. In the Revised Standard Version, one of these words is translated *"regulations"* (Hebrews 9:1,10). Another is translated *"tradition"* (1 Corinthians 11:2), a third is translated *"institution"* (1 Peter 2:13), and the fourth word is sometimes translated *"decrees"* (Ephesians 2:15, Colossians 12:14).

Whichever way it is translated, an ordinance is that which has been decreed or appointed. Sometimes it refers to the decrees of God: *"...walking in all the commandments and ordinances of the Lord blameless"* (Luke 1:6). And sometimes it refers to the decrees of men: *"Submit yourselves to every ordinance of man for the Lord's sake"* (1 Peter 2:13).

The word "ordinance" is never used in the New Testament to designate baptism or the Lord's Supper, apart from any other commandment or decree of the Lord. We do not know when in church history that these two practices came to be known as ordinances. Let's briefly discuss several aspects concerning them.

Number of Church Ordinances

Today some churches practice more ordinances than simply the Lord's Supper and baptism. The Roman Catholic Church has seven: baptism, confirmation, the Holy Eucharist (their name for the Lord's Supper), penance, extreme unction, orders, and marriage. A few of the smaller sects observe three ordinances: baptism, the Lord's Supper, and foot washing. The latter rite is based on the words of Christ to His disciples, recorded in John 13:14–15: *"If I then, your Lord and Master, have washed your feet; ye also ought to wash one another's feet. For I have given you an example, that ye should do as I have done to you."*

> ## Foot washing as an ordinance of the church is doubtful.

Foot washing as an ordinance of the church is doubtful. It is disputed because the early church never observed it. We have a record of the observance of the ordinances of baptism and the Lord's Supper many times, but there is never a mention of foot washing. When the foot washing took place with Jesus, the disciples had been quarreling about who was to be greatest in the kingdom of God. Jesus gave them an example of humble service when He stooped down and washed their feet, since foot washing was a duty that was usually performed by servants. In Jesus' time, foot washing was an act of hospitality and had no religious significance. Jesus was modeling humility to His disciples.

Most of the Protestant bodies agree that just two ordinances were observed by the early churches: baptism and the Lord's Supper. These practice were administered by the authority of the church and under the supervision of the church. It is true that there is no definite command in the New Testament that lays this responsibility directly on the church, but it's a natural deduction that these ordinances are carried out by groups of believers. The command to observe the ordinances was given, not to individuals, but to the groups that composed the nucleus of the church. Jesus was speaking to five hundred people or more when He said, *"Go ye therefore, and teach (make disciples of) all nations, baptizing them in the name of the Father, and of the Son, and of the Holy Ghost"* (Matthew 28:19, addition mine). He was in the upper room with His disciples when He instituted the Lord's Supper. There would be endless confusion if the ordinances were left to individuals.

Nature of the Ordinances

Some people view them as sacraments, imparting spiritual blessing to those who observe them. According to this view, there is saving efficacy in the ordinance of baptism and certain spiritual benefits received in the ordinance of the Lord's Supper. According to the New Testament, the ordinances are symbolic acts that set forth spiritual truths. More will be said about this when we come to consider each ordinances more closely.

Their Purpose

Our Lord did not give arbitrary commands. He always had a gracious purpose. This was true in a special way concerning the ordinances. They are His method of perpetuating the two great heart truths of the gospel: His atoning death and His victorious resurrection. Men might forget these truths and turn to other things. Jesus enshrined these truths in two ordinances, so that they would be kept before the church and the world continually.

The ordinances have been the subject of bitter debate among various religious bodies: some holding one view of their meaning and observance, and some another. New questions have arisen in more modern times that did not arise in the early churches because they were all of one fellowship. There was only one thought in the early church dealing with these questions. Questions of today include alien immersion and open communion. Alien immersion is the idea that a person needs to be rebaptized if they come from a church where they were not fully immersed in water, did not understand the act of baptism properly, or in which their baptism was not carried out by the proper church authority. Open communion refers to the practice of allowing people who are not members of a church to take communion. The whole church does not agree on these questions. They must be settled, not by any direct teaching of the New Testament, but according to the principles laid down in the New Testament and by the practices of the New Testament churches.

Baptism is a critical element of Christianity.

We now come to a more definite consideration of the two ordinances of which Jesus gave specific direction.

BAPTISM

Baptism is a critical element of Christianity. It is through this humbling act that a believer identifies himself or herself with Jesus Christ in a personal and public manner. It is in baptism that we stand before God and mankind, committing to follow Jesus and allow Him to be our Lord and Master. Baptism is a personal declaration by which a person lets their choice be known to the world as they publicly pledge their service and their lives to their Savior. Let's look at baptism as Jesus intended it.

Origin of Baptism

The rite of baptism did not start with Jesus. Gentile converts to Judaism were required to submit to a baptism as a sign of cleansing. Two baptisms in the Bible are given prominence.

Baptism of John the Baptist

When John the Baptist appeared on the scene, he gave a new significance to baptism. Repentance and confession of sin were required of those who sought baptism at his hands. *"And were baptized of him in Jordan, confessing their sins"* (Matthew 3:6).

"I indeed baptize you with water unto repentance" (Matthew 3:11).

Jesus declared that the baptism of John was divinely authorized: *"The baptism of John, whence was it? from heaven, or of men?..."* (Matthew 21:25). Some have denied that John's baptism was a Christian baptism, but Jesus infers that is was authorized by God. Since John the Baptist was fulfilling a divine mission, his actions were obviously sanctioned by the Father.

Paul had this to say about it: *"John verily baptized with the baptism of repentance, saying unto the people, that they should believe on him which should come after him, that is, on Christ Jesus"* (Acts 19:4). The converts at Ephesus were rebaptized, not because they had been baptized unto John's baptism, but because they showed that they did not understand the full significance of

91

John's baptism. At that time it was not required of the early disciples who were baptized by John that they be rebaptized. The difference between John's baptism and the baptism of our time is that John was baptized on profession of faith in a Savior who had actually and already come. John's baptism was focused on repentance and was of necessity. It was the forerunner of the believer's baptism.

Baptism of Jesus

We have the fullest account of this in Matthew 3:13-17: "Then cometh Jesus from Galilee to Jordan unto John, to be baptized of him. But John forbad him, saying, I have need to be baptized of thee, and comest thou to me?' And Jesus answering said unto him, 'Suffer it to be so now: for thus it becometh us to fulfil all righteousness.' Then he suffered him. And Jesus, when he was baptized, went up straightway out of the water; and lo, the heavens were opened unto him, and he saw the spirit of God descending like a dove, and lighting' upon him: And lo, a voice from heaven, saying, 'This is my beloved Son, in whom I am well pleased.'"

The question naturally arises: Why was Jesus baptized when He had no sins to confess? Jesus answered that question when He said, *"Thus it becometh us to fulfill all righteousness"* (Matthew 3:15). It was an act of obedience on His part as well as submission to His Father. It was the right thing to do. Baptism was a divinely appointed rite, and Jesus, in presenting Himself for baptism, was setting an example. By being baptized, Jesus put His approval on John's ministry, identified Himself with those He came to save, and set an example to believers for all time. It should also be remembered that it was at His baptism that heaven gave witness to who He was: the Holy Spirit came and rested upon Him and the Father spoke, affirming Jesus' identity as His Son as well as His approval on Jesus' actions. *"This is my beloved son, in whom I am well pleased"* (Matthew 3:17) is powerful. Jesus' ministry on earth is unleashed. From this time forward, Jesus begins to walk out His purpose outlined in Isaiah 61:1-3:

"The Spirit of the Lord God is upon me; because the Lord hath anointed me to preach good tidings unto the meek; he hath sent me to bind up the brokenhearted, to proclaim liberty to the captives, and the opening of the prison to them that are bound; to proclaim the acceptable year of the Lord, and the day of vengeance of our God; to comfort all that mourn; to appoint unto them that mourn in Zion, to give unto them beauty for ashes, the oil of joy for mourning, the garment of praise for the spirit of heaviness; that they might be called trees of righteousness, the planting of the Lord, that he might be glorified."

Nothing would ever be the same again. Praise the Lord!

The Act of Baptism: Go to the Book!

The method of baptism has been a subject of much controversy among Christians, and much of the controversy has not been very Christian. There is only one place to find the right answer to the question: in the Word of God. Everyone who studies the New Testament with an open heart and unprejudiced mind will agree that New Testament baptism was full immersion in water. This is the meaning of the word in the Greek language, in which the New Testament was written. "Baptism" is not a translation, but a transliteration, of the Greek word *baptisma*[10] which all standard Greek lexicons define as meaning "immersion" or "submersion."

The description of baptism as given in the New Testament requires full immersion: *"...and they were baptized of him in Jordan"*

---

10 "Strongs's #908: baptisma - Greek/Hebrew Definitions - Bible Tools," Strongs's #908: baptisma - Greek/Hebrew Definitions - Bible Tools, accessed January 05, 2017, http://www.bibletools.org/index.cfm/fuseaction/Lexicon.show/ID/G908/baptisma.htm.

(Matthew 3:6).

"And Jesus, when He was baptized, went up straightway out of the water" (Matthew 3:16).

"And they went down both into the water, both Philip and the eunuch, and he baptized him. And when they were come out of the water, the Spirit of the Lord caught away Philip..." (Acts 8:38–39).

The symbolism behind baptism is further evidence that full immersion is the intent of Scripture. The apostle Paul wrote to the church at Rome: *"Therefore we are buried with him by baptism into death: that like as Christ was raised up from the dead by the glory of the Father, even so we also should walk in the newness of life. For if we have been planted together in the likeness of His death, certainly we shall also be in the likeness of His resurrection"* (Romans 6:4–5). Baptism requires a burial in water and a raising up out of that water, a clear picture of immersion.

The symbolism of baptism demands that the subjects be believers. Baptism symbolized a spiritual experience described as death to sin and resurrection to a new life in Christ. For one to be baptized who has not had that experience is to make a mockery of the ordinance.

"And Crispus, the chief ruler of the synagogue, believed on the Lord with all his house: and many of the Corinthians hearing believed, and were baptized" (Acts 18:8). Many other passages could be quoted.

In Scripture, there is no support for infant baptism. Baptism and infants are never mentioned together. Today many parents dedicate their children. This would probably never have started if those who practiced infant baptism had not spoken of the rite as the dedication of their children to the Lord. Primarily the parent's decision, the wisdom of making it a church ceremony is doubtful. The passage of Scripture most often quoted in support of the practice is 1 Samuel 1:11 in which Hannah dedicated her son, Samuel, to the Lord. However, this dedication took place before the child was born. She did not take him to the house of the Lord until he was old enough to be left there. By taking him to Eli the priest and leaving him there to serve, she was only carrying out the vow she had already made when she petitioned God for a child. The other Scripture often referenced for this is Luke 2:22 regarding the dedication of Jesus in the temple. This is also not the same as what churches today practice as it involved animal sacrifice.

> Some hold that baptism is essential to salvation.

Dedication can never take the place of baptism though, and carries no guarantee of salvation. As practiced today, it is simply a public declaration of the intent of parents to raise their child in the Lord. Dedication does not make children Christians as they are not old enough to make their own choice. It is a parental commitment. When that child matures, they must still choose to follow Jesus and get baptized.

Design of Baptism

Some hold that baptism is essential to salvation. In other words, a believer who was not baptized and died would not go to heaven. Many believers in Pentecost have been accused of this. In fact, this idea is the reason infant baptism began.

In support of this view of baptism, several passages of Scripture are offered. One is John 3:5: *"Jesus answered, Verily, verily, I say* unto thee, except a man be born of water and the Spirit, he cannot enter the kingdom of God." It is not at all certain that Jesus was making any reference to baptism in this statement. Some interpreters take the grounds that He was speaking of physical birth when He said *"born of water."* A child is carried in a sac of water which breaks before they are born. If Jesus was referring to baptism here, it was in a symbolic way. Other passages are as follows:

"Repent, and be baptized every one of you in the name of Jesus Christ for the remission of sins..." (Acts 2:38).

"And now why tarriest thou? Arise, and be baptized, and wash away thy sins, calling on the name of the Lord" (Acts 22:16).

"The like figure whereunto even baptism doth also now save us (not the putting away of the filth of the flesh, but the answer of a good conscience toward God) by the resurrection of Jesus Christ" (1 Peter 3:21).

Many men of God have studied

Concerning Acts 2:38, Dr. A. T. Robertson says, "I understand Peter to be urging baptism on each of them who had already turned (repented) and for it to be done in the name of Jesus Christ on the basis of the forgiveness of sins which they had already received." Of Acts 22:16 he says, "Baptism here pictures the washing away of sin by the blood of Christ." And concerning 1 Peter 3:21, he makes these comments: "The saving by baptism which Peter mentions is only symbolic...not actual as Peter hastens to explain... Peter's explanation does not wash away the filth of the flesh either in a literal sense, as a bath for the body, or in a metaphorical sense of the filth of the soul." Baptism does not save us; we get baptized to proclaim the inner miracle that has already taken place in our hearts.

To make baptism essential to salvation is to render salvation partly dependent on works, and not by grace alone, an error which Paul combated powerfully. He insisted that salvation was by grace and works had nothing to do with it. Concerning his own mission, he said, *"For Christ sent me not to baptize, but to preach the gospel"* (1 Corinthians 1:17). Baptism is an outworking of our salvation, but not necessary to secure it.

Baptism symbolizes three truths: the burial and resurrection of Christ, the believer's death to sin, and the resurrection of our bodies when Jesus comes. When a believer gets baptized, they aren't just getting wet or taking part in a dead ritual. They are presenting a picture to the entire congregation of their consecration to Christ as they go under the water (burial and death to sin) and are then raised out of it (their belief in their coming resurrection). Baptism, when properly administered, is one of the most beautiful and impressive services of the church, and should be given the dignity it deserves.

THE LORD'S SUPPER

Four accounts of the institution of the Lord's Supper are given in the Bible. They are found in Matthew 26:26–29, Mark 14:22–25, Luke 22:17–20, and 1 Corinthians 11:23–26. It would be a good idea to review these passages before continuing unless you are already very familiar with them.

Meaning of the Lord's Supper

As Jesus gave the broken bread to His disciples, He said, *"Take, eat; this is my body"* (Matthew 26:26). Likewise, as He gave them the cup, He said, "For this is my blood of the new testament, which is shed for many for the remission of sins" (Matthew 26:28).

The Roman Catholic Church interprets these words literally. It teaches that the bread and wine are actually changed into the very body and blood of Christ by priestly consecration. This is known as transubstantiation which means there is a change into another substance. (Catholic doctrine also believes that there is constant offering for sin in the Eucharist.) The Lutherans and High Church groups hold a somewhat modified view. Lutherans hold that while the elements were not actually changed into the body and blood of

Jesus died once for all.

Christ, but that the body and blood of Christ become present in them when the believer takes them. This is called consubstantiation. Calvin did not agree that the real presence of the body and blood of Christ was in the elements; he held that they were dynamically present and strengthened the believer. All of these views make of the ordinance a sacrament, imparting spiritual blessings to those who partake. One other Reformer did not agree with any of the rest. Zwingli believed the Lord's Supper was symbolic only. His understanding was closest to what the Word of God actually says.

According to the New Testament, the Lord's Supper is simply a memorial of the Lord's death, the bread and wine symbolizing His body and blood. Jesus said, *"This do in remembrance of me"* (1 Corinthians 11:24).

Paul added these words: *"For as often as ye eat this bread, and drink this cup, ye do shew the Lord's death till he come"* (1 Corinthians 11:26). Just as the Passover was a memorial of the deliverance from Egyptian bondage through the blood of the Lamb, so the Lord's Supper is a memorial of the redemption from sin through the atoning death of Christ. It is not a continual sacrifice though as Catholic doctrine believes. This idea would render the Lord's Supper similar to the Old Testament temple worship and suggest that mankind's salvation was dependent on this act. Jesus died once for all. Nothing else is necessary. As He said on the cross, *"It is finished."*

The Lord's Supper is an opportunity for believers to reverence together the work of the Lord on their behalf. It is a time for thankfulness and introspection. We have a God who offered Himself for us, so that we might live. As we take the bread and the wine, we proclaim that we are his and are eagerly awaiting His coming.

Some mainline denominations have been criticized because of their practice of so-called unrestricted Communion. There is really no such thing as unrestricted Communion. Some place more restriction on the Lord's Supper than others, but all denominations put some restriction on it. Some churches are simply more liberal in their practices than others. There are three prerequisites to partaking of the Lord's Supper found in Scripture.

Regeneration

The very meaning of the Lord's Supper requires that only regenerated persons partake of it. It would be mockery for unsaved people to take part in such a sacred ordinance. It is quite evident that Judas had gone from the upper room before Jesus instituted the supper. It was while Jesus and His disciples were eating the Passover that He said, *"Verily I say unto you, that one of you shall betray me"* (Matthew 26:21). When the disciples asked who it was, Jesus replied. *"He it is to whom I shall give a sop, when I have dipped it..."* (John 13:26). Then Jesus dipped the sop and gave it to Judas Iscariot. And John adds, *"He then having received the sop went immediately out..."* (John 13:30).

From that point on, Jesus takes the truth of the Passover and gives it another, deeper layer of meaning. The disciples did not understand it at the time, but after Jesus' resurrection, they understood what He was trying to say to them. The Lord's Supper became a regular part of their times together—as they did this *"in remembrance of"* Him. This is evident by its mention in Paul's letters and by our knowledge of early church practices. It continued to be a central part of Christian worship from then until today.

Baptism

The ordinance of baptism was instituted long before the Lord's Supper. In the Great Commission, Jesus put baptism immediately following conversion, then the observance of the things He had commanded. The record shows that only baptized believers partook of the Lord's Supper in the New Testament churches.

Church Membership

If the Lord's Supper is an ordinance of the church, to be administered by the church, the natural inference is that it is to be administered only to those who are believers, and therefore church members.

This also means that those who have had a conversion experience are acceptable to God. Some Christians refuse to partake of the supper on the grounds that they are not worthy, basing this on the words of Paul: *"Wherefore whosoever shall eat this bread, and drink this cup of the Lord, unworthily, shall be guilty of the body and blood of the Lord"* (1 Corinthians 11:27). This is a misunderstanding of Paul's meaning. If it were a question of being worthy, none of us would partake. Paul was not talking about being worthy but of partaking of the supper in an unworthy manner, in a way morally out of keeping with the nature and design of the ordinance. He was directing them to examine themselves, and did not intend for them to avoid the Lord's Supper. The blood and body of Christ is precious so we should take the time to make sure that we are living a holy Christian life, rightly related to God. This is actually much more serious than we often think it is. Paul wrote that some had died because they failed to discern the body. Therefore the Lord's Supper is a time when we should take the time to allow the Holy Spirit to shine His light on any area that needs change in our heart. Are we walking in sin? Are we walking in unforgiveness? Repentance is an ongoing part of a Christian's life. The Lord's Supper offers an opportunity to repent and recommit our lives to Jesus Christ.

Design

Our Lord gave the Lord's Supper to commemorate His atoning death on the cross. Just as baptism was designed to show the burial and resurrection of Christ, so the supper was designed to show His death on the cross. Just as baptism symbolizes the death of the believer to sin and his or her resurrection to a new life, so the Lord's Supper symbolizes the truth that salvation brings when one partakes through faith of the atonement. Jesus said, *"Verily, verily, I say unto you, except ye eat the flesh of the Son of man and drink his blood, ye have no life in you"* (John 6:53). Baptism, symbolizing the new birth, is observed just once, while the Lord's Supper is repeated often, signifying that one's spiritual life is maintained and strengthened by continued fellowship with Christ.

Frequency

No definite rule is established in the New Testament as to the frequency with which the ordinance is to be observed. One passage would indicate that it was observed daily in the church at Jerusalem: *"And they, continuing daily with one accord in the temple, and breaking bread from house to house, did eat their meat with gladness and singleness of heart"* (Acts 2:46). While breaking bread usually had reference to the observance of the supper, it is not at all clear that this is the meaning in this verse. The American Standard Version reads, *"breaking bread at home."* It probably referred to the regular meal.

In the church at Troas, the supper seems to have been observed each week on the Lord's Day: *"And upon the first day of the week, when the disciples came together to break bread, Paul preached unto them..."* (Acts 20:7). In giving directions about the observance of the supper, Paul said, *"For as often as ye eat this bread, and drink this cup, ye do shew the Lord's death till he come"* (1 Corinthians 11:26). He did not specify how often. That seems to have been left for the individual congregation to decide. If observed too frequently, it may become commonplace, a mere formal service. If not observed often enough, it would lose its importance.

> # The Lord's Supper keeps us focused on the work of the cross.

Our forefathers may have placed too much emphasis on the importance of the Lord's Supper and baptism, but the tendency today is to esteem them too lightly. The ordinances set forth the heart of the gospel message; therefore, they should have an important place in the service of the church. Thoughtful care should be taken in preparing for the observance of the ordinances so that they may be as sacred and powerful as possible. They are not mere ritual, but times in which we proclaim our commitment (in the case of baptism) and remember with grateful hearts why Jesus came to earth in the first place (in the case of

Communion). Both of these practices work toward the edification of the body of Christ. Baptism provides an opportunity to publicly make our intentions known, after which we may be held accountable to our confession in the body. The Lord's Supper keeps us focused on the work of the cross, our common ground. May both be done in holiness and the fear of the Lord.

STUDY QUESTIONS FOR CHAPTER SIX: CHURCH ORDINANCES

1. Which ordinances were clearly practiced by the early church? Which one came first?

2. Concerning baptism, why does only full immersion agree with the Scripture?

3. Why is full immersion important and what does it picture?

4. What, if any, are the prerequisites for baptism?

5. Is baptism essential to salvation? Why or why not?

6. Most Protestants believe the Lord's Supper is purely symbolic. Why or why not do you believe this is true?

7. In 1 Corinthians 11:26 Paul writes, *"For as often as ye eat this bread, and drink this cup, ye do shew the Lord's death till he come."* Using this and other Scriptures, discuss what this means. Why does it not suggest that the Lord's Supper is a continual sacrifice?

8. Discuss what it means to *"eat this bread, and drink this cup of the Lord, unworthily"* (1 Corinthians 11:27). Paul exhorts his reader to "examine" themselves. How do we examine ourselves correctly? Discuss this process and why it is critical to the Christian walk.

9. Discuss Dr. Scott's last point regarding the manner in which we regard these two ordinances and how they are practiced in the church. Do you agree with him? Why or why not?

Chapter 7

Our Worship

Four Greek words in the New Testament translate as "worship." One is *sebomai*[11] which implies fear: *"But in vain do they worship me..."* (Matthew 15:9). A second word is *latreuó*[12] which refers more especially to outward rites and ceremonies, to serving God: *"him only shalt thy serve."* (Matthew 4:10). Another word is *threskeia*[13] which also refers to external acts of worship: *"Let no man beguile you of your reward in a voluntary humility and worshipping of angels..."* (Colossians 2:18). The fourth word, and the one most commonly used, is *proskuneo*[14] which means to make obeisance, to prostrate oneself: *"For we have seen his star in the east, and are come to worship him"* (Matthew 2:2). As these words make clear,

---

11 "Strongs's #4576: sebomai - Greek/Hebrew Definitions - Bible Tools," Strongs's #4576: sebomai - Greek/Hebrew Definitions - Bible Tools, accessed January 04, 2017, http://www. bibletools.org/index.cfm/fuseaction/Lexicon.show/ID/G4576/sebomai.htm.

12 "Strong's Greek: 3000. (latreuó) – to serve," Strong's Greek: 3000. (latreuó) – to serve, accessed January 04, 2017, http://biblehub.com/greek/3000.htm.

13 "Strongs's #2356: threskeia - Greek/Hebrew Definitions - Bible Tools," Strongs's #2356: threskeia - Greek/Hebrew Definitions - Bible Tools, accessed January 04, 2017, http://www. bibletools.org/index.cfm/fuseaction/Lexicon.show/ID/G2356/threskeia.htm.

14 "Strongs's #4352: proskuneo - Greek/Hebrew Definitions - Bible Tools," Strongs's #4352: proskuneo - Greek/Hebrew Definitions - Bible Tools, accessed January 04, 2017, http://www. bibletools.org/index.cfm/fuseaction/Lexicon.show/ID/G4352/proskuneo.htm.

the act of worship pertains to more than following the order of a service, although that is certainly an important part of it. As in all else, we much achieve a balance.

THE NATURE OF WORSHIP

Worship is intended to be done in reverence to God. *Our worship is our entire service to God.* Man's purpose is to worship God. An act of worship includes anything that is done out of reverence for God, and that covers a lot.

Worship does not only refer to a song service; our singing is only part of our worship. There is a reason we associate worship with praise though. Scripture says that God's people overflow in praise to their God and that He, in turn, *"inhabitest the praises of Israel"* (Psalm 22:3). In his book, *When the Song Begins*, J. R. Miller likened our worship to a song that begins from the moment we are first converted and infused with the love of Jesus. He wrote that the danger of formal religion was that Christians could go "through a course of formal service, but they are never be happy in it, are never enthusiastic followers of Christ...they have just a little religion, enough to make life harder in the way of restraint and limitation, but not enough to start the song. They measure their piety, they calculate their service, they know nothing of full abandonment to Christ." Then he says, "Only in entire surrender and devotion to Christ can we learn to sing the new song." Our song rises from our hearts and permeates all we are and all we do.

Both an Inward Experience and an Outward Experience

True worship is a spiritual exercise. To the woman at the well, Jesus revealed the heart of true worship: *"But the hour cometh, and now is, when the true worshippers shall worship the Father in spirit* and in truth; for the Father seeketh such to worship him. *God is a Spirit: and they that worship him must worship him in spirit and in truth"* (John 4:23–24). It is natural to give outward expression in praise and prayer, but there may be worship without these. One worships when others are provided for by God through us under His direction. One also worships when his or her heart is lifted to God in reverence and gratitude. The outward acts of worship mean nothing to God unless they are the expression of that inward state. Much that is called worship among people is not worship in the eyes of God. It's before the eyes of God that our worship is truly measured.

Brother Lawrence in his Christian classic, *Practicing the Presence of God*, written in the fifteenth century, had this to say, "...we ought not to be weary of doing little things for the love of God, who regards not the greatness of the work, but the love with which it is performed." He is speaking specifically about what we do for God, but he touches on the crux of the matter. Our worship is an outworking of our love for Jesus, within and without. Sometimes it is heard in the clear tones of music. Other times it is seen in our care for others, friend and stranger alike. Sometimes it is in the privacy of our hearts and between us and God alone. Sometimes it flows in prayer, and other times it is completely silent, prostrate before God.

Our worship is an outworking of our love for Jesus, within and without.

Private or Public

One may worship God alone or with other Christians. A person may worship in the home, in the field, in the forest, or in the house of the Lord. A person may worship at any time or at an appointed time. People who do not worship God in private are not likely to worship Him in the church.

This does not mean that private worship can take the place of public worship. Some professing Christians give as an excuse for not attending the services of God's house that they can worship God at home or out in the field just as well as they can at the place of public worship. But the truth is, they cannot. There is something to be gained, and something to be given, in public worship that cannot be gained or given anywhere else. God has appointed worship in all of His churches as a means by which His people may grow in the grace and knowledge of the Lord Jesus Christ and may impart spiritual benefits to others. He warns against neglect of this sacred privilege and responsibility: *"And let us consider one another to provoke unto love and to good works: not forsaking the assembling of ourselves together, as the manner of some is: but exhorting one another; and so much the more, as ye see the day approaching"* (Hebrews 10:24–25). So private worship should never be practiced exclusively. Every believer should be rightly related to God and rightly related to the body of Christ. We cannot maintain good spiritual health without both.

Not a Replacement for Work

The two go together, worship and work. We worship God, proud of the gospel, in every facet of our lives. One cannot worship aright unless he or she is willing to work, and one cannot work aright until he or she has worshipped. Worship cannot be made a substitute for work, and work cannot be made a substitute for worship. In the early and Middle Ages of the Christian era, there arose a class of so-called saints who were known as Stylites or Pillar Saints. They erected pillars of varying heights and spent their years perched on top of these pillars. God wants no pillar saints. His program calls for worship and work.

THE FORM OF WORSHIP

There seems to have been no set form of worship in the New Testament churches. Their worship was marked by simplicity. There was no elaborate ritual such as that characterized by the temple worship of the Old Testament and by the worship of some churches today. There was a freedom about it that was sometimes carried to excess, as in the church at Corinth, where congregants were shouting and all speaking with tongues at the same time. Paul had to exhort them to see that *"all things be done decently and in order"* (1 Corinthians 14:40).

Many churches of today are in danger of going to the other extreme—laying too much stress on form. Programs for the services are made up days ahead, and they vary very little from week to week. There is a time to sing, a time to read, a time to pray, and so on. Thought should be given to the order of worship certainly. Programs have their place, but they are to be the servants, not the masters.

Reverend Starke, a minister of another generation stated the truth in these words: "No service of God can be without ceremonies; but that is the most excellent which has cast off external parade and has most of the Spirit."[15]

There was no set form of worship on the day of Pentecost, but the lambency or radiance was there: *"And they were all filled with*

---

15 Johann Peter Lange, Commentary on the Holy Scriptures (New York: Scribner, 1884).

the Holy Spirit and began to speak with other tongues, as the Ghost was giving them utterance" (Acts 2:4).

There was no set form of worship in the church at Jerusalem, either, but again, the lambency was there: *"And when they had prayed, the place was shaken where they were assembled together; and they were all filled with the Holy Ghost, and they spake the word of God with boldness"* (Acts 4:31). It is all right to have forms of worship, but we must be sure the brilliance of the Holy Spirit is displayed.

THE PLACE OF WORSHIP

The church at Jerusalem first met in the famous upper room: *"And when they were come in, they went up into an upper room"* (Acts 1:13).

For a time, they seemed to have gone to the temple for worship: *"And they, continuing daily with one accord in the temple..."* (Acts 2:46). In their missionary work, the apostles usually went to the Jewish synagogues.

When driven from those, they went into public buildings and private homes. Many of the churches met in private homes. In closing his epistle to the church at Colosse, Paul sent this greeting: *"Salute the brethren which are in Laodicea, and Nymphas, and the church which is in his house"* (Colossians 4:15).

And to his friend Philemon he wrote, *"Unto Philemon our dearly beloved, and fellow labourer, And to our beloved Apphia, and Archippus our fellow soldier, and to the church in thy house"* (Philippians 1:1–2).

When persecution became severe, the churches were driven

to worship in secret places. The Christians at Rome made use of the catacombs (underground burying places) for the purpose of worship. It was not until the first half of the third century that houses of worship were erected.

It is necessary that churches have places in which to worship. In more modern times, there have been two extremes in church architecture: Some, in their stinginess, have been satisfied with ugly shacks, while others, in their pride, have built for show. Two things should characterize church buildings: utility and beauty. Some churches have sacrificed utility for beauty, and some have sacrificed beauty for utility. There is no reason why houses of worship should not be both beautiful and useful.

> # The true place of worship is in our hearts.

However, the bottom line is that the true place of worship is in our hearts. The building is just a building. We're the real building. Worship springs from the hearts of God's people wherever they are as they worship Him *"in spirit and truth."* Our focus should be on the beauty of the presence of Jesus which inhabits the body of Christ. We should use whatever building God has given us to glorify and honor Him, and be thankful for it.

THE TIME OF WORSHIP

It seems that for a time, the church at Jerusalem met daily for worship: *"And they, continuing daily with one accord in the temple..."* (Acts 2:46). Many of the Jewish Christians continued to worship on the seventh day of the week, the Jewish Sabbath.

But before the close of the apostolic period, the first day of the week, called the Lord's Day, became the day of worship: *"Upon the first day of the week let every one of you lay by him in store, as God hath prospered him..."* (1 Corinthians 16:2).

"I was in the Spirit on the Lord's day..." (Revelation 1:10).

It was on the first day of the week that our Lord arose from the dead. It is fitting, therefore, that this day, the Lord's Day, should have been chosen by the early Christians, under the leadership of the Holy Spirit, as their day of worship.

The Roman Catholic Church claims to have changed the day of worship from the seventh to the first day of the week. But this change came long before there was a Roman Catholic Church. Justin Martyr, writing in about AD 150 said, "On Sunday all the Christians, living either in the city or country, met together."[16] Although we meet on Sundays congregationally and worship the Lord, this does not preclude the fact that we worship the Lord throughout the week too.

THE PARTS OF WORSHIP

There were five distinct elements in the worship of the New Testament churches. They are prayer, praise, reading the Scriptures, teaching and exhortation, and the offering. Every one of these disciplines can be practiced individually as well as corporately, and should be.

Prayer

Prayer occupied a very prominent place in the worship of the early churches. More is said about their praying than about any other part of their worship.

16 W. Goodhugh and W. C. Taylor, The Bible cyclopaedia: or, Illustrations of the civil and natural history of the sacred writings (London: J.W. Parker, 1841), 782.

No Set Form

It is significant that the Lord's Prayer is not mentioned in the New Testament except in the Gospels. It was meant as a model for prayer, not as a scripted prayer. It seems not to have been in general use in the worship of the churches. *Prayer was the free and spontaneous expression of the feelings and desires of the heart.*

No Prescribed Attitude

In the garden of Gethsemane, Jesus fell on His face and prayed: *"And he went a little further, and fell on his face, and prayed... "*(Matthew 26:39). In the instructions concerning prayer that He gave to His disciples, Jesus said, "And when ye stand praying..." (Mark 11:25). Paul wrote to Timothy, urging *"that men pray every where, lifting up holy hands, without wrath and doubting"* (1 Timothy 2:8). Paul also spoke of bowing the knees in prayer (Ephesians 3:14)—all of which means that prayer is not a physical exercise. A person may pray in any position that suits them.

There are many aspects of prayer. Sometimes our prayer only focuses on one of them. Other times it uses several or even all of them. Our prayer may be a simple invocation, calling on God to hear. Such was the prayer of David: *"Hear, O Lord, when I cry with my voice: have mercy also upon me, and answer me"* (Psalm 27:7).

It may be adoration, paying homage to a holy God: *"Thou art worthy, O Lord, to receive glory and honor and power..."* (Revelation 4:11).

It may be thanksgiving, expressing gratitude to God for His blessings: *"Bless the Lord, O my soul: and all that is within me, bless his holy name. Bless the Lord, O my soul, and forget not all his benefits"* (Psalm. 103:1–2).

Or it may be confession, asking God to forgive sin: "Have mercy upon me, O God, according to thy lovingkindness; according unto the multitude of thy tender mercies blot out my transgressions…For I acknowledge my transgressions: and my sin is ever before me" (Psalm 51:1, 3).

We may intercede, or appeal to God in behalf of others: *"I exhort therefore, that, first of all, supplications, prayer, intercessions, and giving of thanks, be made for all men"* (1 Timothy 2:1). This is the one thing Jesus is doing for us in heaven. Hebrews 7:25 states: *"Wherefore he is able also to save them to the uttermost that come unto God by him, seeing he ever liveth to make intercession for them."*

> # Prayer is as unique and individual as God's people.

We may petition God, asking God for certain blessings and help. Paul asked for prayer that he might *"be delivered from the unbelievers in Judea, and that my service for Jerusalem may be acceptable to the saints"* (Romans 15:31 RSV). He also prayed for the church at Ephesus that they might receive *"a spirit of wisdom and of revelation in the knowledge of him (God), having the eyes of your hearts enlightened, that you may know what is the hope to which he has called you, what are the riches of his glorious inheritance in the saints"* (Ephesians 1:17, 18 RSV).

Prayer is as unique and individual as God's people. It would be impossible to relate every facet of prayer in these short pages, but the point is that prayer was a vital part of the early church. The place and power of prayer are exemplified in Scripture. It was while the disciples were praying in the upper room that Pentecostal power came: *"These all continued with one accord in prayer and supplication"* (Acts 1:14). It was while the church was at prayer that *"the place was shaken where they were assembled together; and they were all filled with the Holy Ghost, and they space the word of God with boldness"* (Acts 4:31). It was while the church was in prayer that the angel of the Lord came down, and opened prison doors, and set Peter free: *"Peter therefore was kept in prison: but prayer was made without ceasing of the church unto God for him"* (Acts 12:5). Prayer should continue to hold a prominent place in our churches today.

Prayer changes things! It changes us and it changes the circumstances around us. For every Christian, then and now, prayer is, and always will be, a vital part of our faith. Nothing can stop us from praying as it does not have to be out loud. When we pray, God hears us, speaks to us, and answers us. It is through this connection that we are continually refreshed in the presence of the Lord.

Praise

Praise may be expressed in various ways, but we usually associate it with song. It is an important part of worshiping God. Many of the psalms are songs of praise. The worship in both the temple and later, in synagogues, was characterized by praise. It was only natural, then, that praise should have an important place in the worship of the church. Just before Jesus and His disciples left the upper room to go to Gethsemane, they sang a hymn: *"And when they had sung an hymn, they went out..."* (Mark 14:26). While Paul and Silas lay with bleeding backs in the jail at Philippi, they *"prayed, and sang praises unto God..."* (Acts 16:25). The fact that songs of praise were a part of the worship of the churches is shown by the words of Paul to the Ephesians:

"Speaking to yourselves in psalms and hymns and spiritual songs..." (Ephesians 5:19).

"Teaching and admonishing one another in all wisdom, and singing psalms, hymns, and spiritual songs..." (Colossians 3:16).

Emphasis was placed on the spirit of praise rather than on its outward expression. It was not formal music rendered to win the praise of men. Church services were not performance-based. It was music that came from the heart: *"I will sing with the spirit, and I will sing with the understanding also"* (Ephesians 5:19), and *"...singing with grace in your hearts to the Lord"* (Colossians 3:16). What would Paul say of churches that employed singers because they have trained voices, but give little evidence of Christian character?

Instrumental music had a prominent place in the worship of the temple. Musical instruments may have been used in the worship of the early churches, but we have no record of it. However, many instruments are mentioned in regard to Old Testament worship, so we know instruments were a familiar part of their cultural experience.

Reading the Scriptures

Reading the Scriptures occupied a large place in the worship of the synagogues too, and the churches seem to have continued this practice. Of course, the only Scriptures the early churches had were those of the Old Testament. Paul exhorted young Timothy to *"give attendance to reading"* (1 Timothy 4:13). The Word of God was the weapon with which the churches were to win victories: *"For the word of God is quick, and powerful, and sharper than any two-edged sword, piercing even to the dividing asunder of soul and spirit, and of the joints and marrow, and is a discerner of the thoughts and intents of the heart"* (Hebrews 4:12).

Jesus read the Scriptures when he attended synagogue, and all the disciples would have been familiar with this ancient practice. Their reverence for the Word of God was a cultural part of their DNA. Once the Holy Spirit indwelled them, He began to fulfill His divine mission: *"But the Counselor, the Holy Spirit, whom the Father will send in my name, he will teach you all things, and bring to your remembrance all that I have said to you"* (John 14:26 RSV). Being able to understand the Word of God was a necessary part of this process.

"All scripture is given by inspiration of God, and is profitable for doctrine, for reproof, for correction, for instruction in righteousness" (2 Timothy 3:16). The Scriptures are described as the instruments of regeneration, quickening, illumination, sanctification, cleansing, comforting, and so much more. We may be sure that the Christian churches made much of reading the Scriptures.

> Christian churches made much of reading the Scriptures.

Teaching and Exhortation

Along with the reading of the Scriptures, there was usually an explanation of what was read. Jesus did that in the synagogue at Nazareth when He told His hearers that He was fulfilling the Word of God. Later Paul and Barnabas, who were attending the worship of the synagogue at Antioch, were called to speak following the reading of the Scriptures: *"And after the reading of the law and the prophets the rulers of the synagogue sent unto them, saying, Ye men and brethren, if ye have any word of exhortation for the people, say on"* (Acts 13:15). The public testimony in the churches took various forms, such as prophesying, exhortations, tongues and interpretations, and so on. Sometimes a number of people spoke at the same time, creating confusion in the service. Paul rebuked the church at Corinth, saying: *"If any thing be revealed to another that sitteth by, let the first hold his peace. For ye may all prophesy one by one, that all may learn, and all may be comforted...For God is not the author of confusion, but of peace, as in all churches of the saints"* (1 Corinthians 14:30, 33).

As churches grew and multiplied, preaching became more prominent. Jesus had commissioned His disciples to go and preach the gospel. When the Christians were driven from Jerusalem by persecution, they *"went every where preaching the word"* (Acts 8:4).

Paul made much of preaching, and the burden of his message was the cross of Christ: *"But we preach Christ crucified..."* (1 Corinthians 1:23). He gave as the heart of the gospel that he was commissioned to preach: *"How that Christ died for our sins according to the scriptures; and that he was buried, and that he rose again the third day according to the scriptures"* (1 Corinthians 15:3–4). His injunction to Timothy was *"Preach the word..."* (2 Timothy 4:2). God has offered no substitute for preaching, and He has offered no substitute for the subject of the message.

The Offering

The offering was another element that gradually found a place in the worship of the church. The church at Jerusalem had a community of goods. Some of those who had possessions sold them and put the proceeds into the common fund, but there was nothing compulsory about it. As the Christians spread out and new churches were organized, the taking of offerings became more common. The church at Antioch took offerings for the poor saints at Jerusalem. Paul, in his missionary work, called on the churches to make contributions for the needy in other places. In his first epistle to the church at Corinth, he set up a definite plan for giving: *"Upon the first day of the week let every one of you lay by him in store, as God hath prospered him..."* (1 Corinthians 16:2). There has never been found a better plan that that of regular, systematic, proportionate giving on the part of each one for the benefit of the whole.

Paul also stressed the spirit in which the offering is to be made: *"Every man according as he purposeth in his heart, so let him give; not grudgingly, or of necessity: for God loveth a cheerful giver"* (2 Corinthians 9:7). He also emphasized the fact that the gift without the giver is bare: *"...but first gave their own selves to the Lord"* (2 Corinthians 8:5).

> ## God has offered no substitute for preaching.

The taking of the offering is sometimes looked upon as a "necessary evil." It is often covered up and made as painless as possible by music and even a special performance of sorts. But the offering that is given to the Lord as an expression of love and gratitude is as much a part of worship as singing and praying, and should not require such a buffer. We should give to God out of a heart filled with love, literally giving Him back for His use a portion of what He has already given us.

THE PURPOSES OF WORSHIP

There seems to have been a threefold purpose in the worship of the New Testament churches.

Our Growth and Development as Worshippers

New converts are described as babes in Christ. They are to grow and develop in spiritual stature. In the early church, the new converts found Christian fellowship and were grounded in doctrine and instructed in righteousness. *"And he gave some, apostles; and some, prophets; and some, evangelists; and some, pastors and teachers; for the perfecting of the saints, for the work of the ministry, for the edifying of the body of Christ; till we all come in the unity of the faith, and of the knowledge of the Son of God, unto a perfect man, unto the measure of the stature of the fullness of Christ: that we henceforth be no more children, tossed to and fro, and carried about with every wind of doctrine, by the sleight of men, and cunning craftiness, whereby they lie in wait to deceive; but speaking the truth in love, may grow up into him in all things, which is the head, even Christ"* (Ephesians 4:11–15). This process continues today. It is through proper relationship to the body of Christ that a new believer is discipled and grows in a healthy manner.

Winning Others to Christ

In a worshipping church, a spirit and a power are present that profoundly influence the unsaved. The description of such a church is found in 1 Corinthians 14:23–25: *"If therefore the whole church be come together in one place, and all speak with tongues, and there come in those that are unlearned, or unbelievers, will they not say that ye are mad? But if all prophesy, and there come in one that believeth not, or one unlearned, he is convinced of all, he is judged of all: and thus are the secrets of his heart made manifest; said so falling down on his face he will worship God, and, report that God is in you of a truth."* More people are converted in a worshipping church than anywhere else. This is one of the ways that the Holy Spirit witnesses to the world.

Declaration of the Glory of God

The principle laid down in 1 Corinthians 10:30, *"Whether therefore ye eat, or drink, or whatsoever ye do, do all to the glory of God,"* is applicable in a special manner to the worship of the church. Paul's benediction in Ephesians 3:20–21 suggests the same truth: *"Now unto him that is able to do exceeding abundantly above all that we ask or think, according to the power that worketh in us, unto him be glory in the church and in Christ Jesus throughout all ages, world without end. Amen."* When we gather as the body of Christ, we minister to God Himself. The Holy Spirit moves among us and His presence abides with us individually and corporately.

REVERENCE IN WORSHIP

There are two extremes in the attitude of people toward the place of worship. One group almost makes an idol of the church building, while the other group rushes thoughtlessly into the place of worship and acts in a way that destroys any sense of reverence toward God.

Reverence in the house of God was stressed in the Old Testament: *"Ye shall keep my sabbaths, and reverence my sanctuary: I am the Lord"* (Leviticus 26:2).

Not a great deal is said about it specifically in the early church, but Paul rebuked the Christians at Corinth for their unseemly conduct at the Lord's Supper and for the confusion that often existed in their worship. The author of the Hebrews gave this exhortation: *"Wherefore we receiving a kingdom which cannot be moved, let us have grace, whereby we may serve God acceptably with reverence and godly fear"* (Hebrews 12:28). The spirit of reverence is necessary for spiritual worship.

This does not mean we must bow as we enter or spend the service on our knees (although there is nothing wrong with either practice at times). It means that within ourselves we should come to God as He has outlined. God went to a lot of trouble and gave all He had to open the way for mankind to approach Him without falling over dead, as they did in the Old Testament (Exodus 19:12). When we are irreverent, we are not truly appreciating the work of the cross on our behalf. As Scripture tells us *"the fear of the Lord is the beginning of wisdom"* (Proverbs 9:10 RSV). Walking with a healthy reverence individually toward our Father will guide us into His ways and His wisdom, and is vital to our continued growth. As we gather corporately this will result in a greater and stronger sense of His presence among us.

> The spirit of reverence is necessary for spiritual worship.

THE PLACE OF WOMEN IN THE WORSHIP IN THE CHURCH

From the beginning of Christ's ministry, women were active helpers: *"And certain women, which had been healed of evil spirits and infirmities, Mary called Magdalene, out of whom went seven devils, And Joanna the wife of Chuza Herod's steward, and Susanna, and many others, which ministered unto him of their substance"* (Luke 8:2–3). They stood by the cross when Jesus died and did not run away like the disciples did. They also followed His body to the tomb and were the first to discover the open tomb and tell the story of the risen Lord.

It was also to a woman that Jesus first declared Himself as the Messiah: *"I that speak unto thee am he"* (John 4:26).

Women were in the upper room before the day of Pentecost praying with the disciples: *"These all continued with one accord in prayer and supplication, with the women..."* (Acts 1:14). Philip, the deacon and evangelist, had four daughters who prophesied (Acts 21:9).

It was to a group of praying women that Paul came when he crossed over into Macedonia: *"And on the Sabbath we went out of the city by a river side, where prayer was wont to be made; and we sat down and spake unto the women which resorted thither"* (Acts 16:13).

It was a woman who was his first European convert, and in her home he found an abiding place. Years later, when he wrote his epistle to the Philippian church, he spoke of *"those women which labored with me in the gospel"* (Philippian 4:3). He commended Phebe to the church at Rome as *"a servant (deaconess) of the church which is at Cenchrea"* (Romans 16:1, addition mine).

He spoke of the church's unity as one fellowship, without regard to race or sex: *"There is neither Jew nor Greek, there is neither bond nor free, there is neither male nor female: for ye are all one in Christ Jesus"* (Galatians 3:28).

Yet in his letter to the Corinthian church, Paul gave women a secondary place in the worship: *"Let your women keep silence in the churches: for it is not permitted unto them to speak; but they are commanded to be under obedience, as also saith the law. And if they will learn any thing, let them ask their husbands at home: for it is a shame for women to speak in the church"* (1 Corinthians 14:34–35). Again, in his first epistle to Timothy, he wrote, *"Let the woman learn in silence with all subjection. But I suffer not a woman to teach, nor to usurp authority over the man, but to be in silence. For Adam was first formed, then Eve. And Adam was not deceived, but the woman being deceived was in the transgression."* (1 Timothy 2:11–14).

Was Paul taking into consideration the times and customs of that day when he spoke these words, as so were instruction for that time period only? Or were these instructions also meant to address us, and was he laying down a principle for all time? Good Christians—both theologians and laypeople—disagree in their answers to these questions, but all agree that our churches owe much to the devotion and loyal service of women.

STUDY QUESTIONS FOR CHAPTER SEVEN: OUR WORSHIP

1. Dr. Scott writes that *"the outward acts of worship mean nothing to God unless they are the expression of that inward state."* To what inward state is he referring?

2. As we each individually worship God and sing our new song, it impacts the world around us. Discuss the effect of your worship on those around you.

3. The answer to the question as to why God created man is that man is to glorify God and enjoy Him forever. How does our worship glorify God? How do we "enjoy" God?

4. Why is it a mistake to think that, under normal circumstances, you can worship on your own apart from the body and still grow as you should? Why do believers even come to this and what can be done to help them?

5. Why is it a mistake to measure our Christianity by our church attendance? How ought we to measure our devotion to God instead?

6. How is prayer a part of your worship? How much time do you spend with the Lord in prayer daily? Do you notice a correlation between your prayer life and your success as a Christian?

7. When we worship God corporately, something happens. Describe experiences you have had during corporate worship, praising God as a group.

8. The study of the Word is an integral part of worship. This has been modeled to us since the time of temple worship. What are the benefits of studying and reading the Bible? Make a list

together!

9. Teaching and preaching are part of worship too. Consider the importance of both. How are they alike and how are they different? What is the result of each one?

10. What is reverence and why is it *"necessary for spiritual worship"* according to Dr. Scott?

11. Galatians 3:28 says, "There is neither Jew nor Greek, there is neither bond nor free, there is neither male nor female: for ye are all one in Christ Jesus." Discuss the implication on society this verse brings. Compare it with Jesus' words in John 17:9,10 and 17-24.

Chapter 8

Our Mission

Our Lord instituted the church because He had something for it to do in the world. He entrusted to it the responsibility of carrying on His work. The church is described as the body of Christ. Through that body, He does His work. Through the lips of Christians, He speaks. By the hands of Christians, He ministers, and through the feet of Christians, He moves among men. Let's take a closer look at the type of work Christ expects the church to do.

THE NATURE OF THE WORK

What was the work our Lord committed to the church? In 1 Timothy 3:15, we find a reference to *"the church of the living God, the pillar and ground of the truth."* The Revised Standard Version translates it as *"the pillar and bulwark of the truth."* A bulwark is a protective wall.

Friendship

A church should be the friend of all churches: one body called together with a common purpose, but Paul was speaking about revealed truth, the truth as revealed in the Word of God, the truth as it is in Christ Jesus. In His prayer as recorded in the John 17, Jesus said, *"Sanctify them through thy truth."* In John 14:6, Jesus declared, *"I am the way, the truth, and the life..."* The truth that has been entrusted to the church is spiritual truth, the truth about God, the truth about sin, the truth about the person and the work of Christ, the truth about the Holy Spirit, the truth about salvation, and the truth about the world to come. The church is not the source of truth, nor is it the author of truth; it is the guardian and publisher of the truth.

A Guardian of Truth

The church is to guard the truth: *"Beloved, when I gave all diligence to write unto you of the common salvation, it was needful for me to write unto you, and exhort you that ye should earnestly contend for the faith which was once delivered unto the saints. For there are certain men crept in unawares, who were before of old ordained to this condemnation, ungodly men, turning the grace of our God unto lasciviousness, and denying the only Lord God, and our Lord Jesus Christ."* (Jude 1:3–4). This charge is vital to protect the message of the gospel and combat error and heresy.

A Proclaimer of Truth

The church is to proclaim the truth, to publish it abroad. The Lord did not give the truth to the church to be hidden, but to make it known to all men. The words of Paul to Timothy are applicable to the church: *"Study to shew thyself approved unto God, a workman that needeth not to be ashamed, rightly dividing the word of truth"* (2 Timothy 2:15). It is a tragedy when a church becomes the pillar and ground of error instead of the truth, or when it ceases to proclaim its message, hiding its light under a bushel.

The Agent of Christ

Jesus said to His disciples, *"As my Father hath sent me, even so send I you"* (John 20:21).

In His intercessory prayer, He said, *"As thou hast sent me into the world, even so have I also sent them into the world"* (John 17:18). Christ carries on His work in the world through His people, the church. The work of Jesus was twofold.

Our Physical and Material Needs

He fed the hungry, healed the sick, opened the eyes of the blind, cleansed the leper, and enabled the lame to walk. In like manner, Jesus expects His church to minister to the physical needs of men. He said that in doing this, they are ministering to Him: *"Verily I say unto you, in as much as ye have done it unto me"* (Matthew 25:40). He also said that failure to minister to the needy was failure to minister to Him: *"Verily I say unto you, inasmuch as ye did it not unto one of the least of these my brethren, ye have done it unto me"* (Matthew 25:45). Paul urged the churches to care for the poor. John declared that neglect of the needy showed a lack of the love of God in the heart: *"But whoso hath this world's good, and seeth his brother have need, and shutteth up his bowels of compassion from him, how dwelleth the love of God in him?"* (1 John 3:17). And James, the brother of the Lord, said that neglect of the poor revealed a lack of true faith: *"If a brother or sister be naked, and destitute of daily food, and one of you say unto them, Depart in peace, be ye warmed and filled; notwithstanding ye give them not those things which are needful for the body; what doth it profit? Even so faith, if it hath not works, is dead, being alone"* (James 2:15–17).

This was the primary purpose of Jesus coming to the world. He did feed the hungry, heal the sick, and care for the needy, but those things were secondary in His mission. They were ministries along the way. His great purpose in coming to the world was to save the lost: *"For God sent not his Son into the world to condemn the world; but that the world through him might be saved"* (John 3:17). Jesus said of His coming, *"For the Son of man is come to seek and to save that which is lost"* (Luke 19:10). And Paul summed it up in these words: *"This is a faithful saying, and worthy of all acceptation, that Christ Jesus came into the world to save sinners…"* (1 Timothy 1:15). In fact, the redemption of mankind is the overarching theme of the entire Bible.

Winning the lost to Christ is the church's supreme task.

As this was primary in the work of Christ, so it is the first order in the work of the church. In giving His Great Commission, Jesus did not say, *"Go ye therefore and feed the hungry and heal the sick."* He said, *"Go ye therefore and make disciples of all nation"* (Matthew 28:19). Winning the lost to Christ is the church's supreme task.

There are two extremes to which some Christians have gone. There are those who have said, *"Get the people saved; let their physical needs go."* Others have said, *"Minister to the physical and social needs of the world; that is the main task."* Jesus combined the two, putting the spiritual needs first. Sometimes He cared for people's physical needs to open the way for ministering to their spiritual needs.

It was the saving grace of the gospel that put compassion into the hearts of men and kindled the desire to relieve human suffering. The Philippian jailer cared nothing about the suffering of Paul and Silas as he cast them into the inner prison, made their feet fast in the stocks, and left them to suffer. Bust as soon as he found the Savior, he became interested in relieving the suffering men: *"And he took them the same hour of the night, and washed their stripes..."* (Acts 16:33).

There is little compassion for suffering humanity in the world today among people who have not come under the influence of the gospel. It is Christianity that has built the hospitals, orphanages, and homes for the aged and infirmed. That's why so many hospitals have names like Good Samaritan, St. Joseph's or St. Jude's; they were begun by the churches. Such institutions as these are not found in lands that have not been touched by the gospel of Christ.

Although winning the lost to Christ is the main task of the church, it cannot afford to neglect its ministry in other fields. There is a growing tendency to turn this world over to agencies of the government or to departments of social work. The church will lose a great opportunity if it abandons this field.

THE SCOPE OF THE WORK

Where is the church to find its field of labor?

In the Church

The church is to minister to the different needs of its own members. The church should not rely on others to meet their needs.

Physical Needs

The church is to look after the poor among its own members, visit the sick, and share with those who are in need. Again, James the brother of the Lord, speaks: *"Is any sick among you? Let him call for the elders of the church..."* (James 5:14). *"Pure religion and undefiled before God and the Father is this, to visit the fatherless and the widows in their affliction, and to keep himself unspotted from the world"* (James 1:27).

Spiritual Needs

The church is to teach and admonish its members that they may grow in the grace and knowledge of the Lord Jesus Christ: *"Warning every man, and teaching every man in all wisdom; that we may present every man perfect in Christ Jesus"* (Colossians 1:28). The words of Paul in Ephesians 4:11–15, which have already been quoted, are applicable here as well.

The church is to exercise a wholesome discipline over its members. The heart of true discipline is love. The spirit of anger or hate or spite has no place in church discipline. "Brethren, if a man be overtaken in a fault, ye which are spiritual, restore such an one in the spirit of meekness; considering thyself, lest thou also be tempted" (Galatians 6:1). Other version use the word "gentleness" instead of meekness. The church should be flowing in the fruit of the Holy Spirit, and so should be known for their lovingkindness towards their own.

The New Testament mentions two kinds of offenses the church is to deal with:

• **Private Offenses, or Differences among Individual Members:** Jesus outlined the procedure in dealing with these offenses: *"Moreover if thy brother shall trespass against thee, go and tell him his fault between thee and him alone: if he shall hear thee, thou hast gained thy brother. But if he will not hear thee, then take with thee one or two more, that in the mouth of two or three* *witnesses every word may be established. And if he shall neglect to hear them, tell it unto the church: but if he neglect to hear the church, let him be unto thee as an heathen man and a publican"* (Matthew 18:15–17). These problems were to be dealt with responsibly among the members of the church.

Paul upbraided the members of the church at Corinth for going to law with another: *"But brother goeth to law with brother, and that before the unbelievers. Now therefore there is utterly a fault among you, because ye go to law one with another. Why do ye not rather take wrong? Why do ye not rather suffer yourselves to be defrauded?"* (1 Corinthians 6:6–7).

• **Public Offenses:** These are of two kinds: lapses in morals and lapses in doctrine. The church is to deal with members who fall into immorality and members who depart from sound doctrine. In the spirit of love, the church is to make an effort to reclaim those who have fallen. If they persist in their evil ways, the church is to withdraw fellowship from them. Concerning the member of the Corinthian church who was guilty of gross immorality, Paul said, *"Put away from among yourselves that wicked person"* (1 Corinthians 5:13). And with regard to those who had departed from the faith in the church at Thessalonica, he gave this urgent

> The church is to teach and admonish its members that they may grow in the grace and knowledge of the Lord Jesus Christ.

counsel: *"Now we command you, brethren, in the name of the Lord Jesus Christ, that ye withdraw yourselves from every brother that walketh disorderly, and not after the tradition which he received of us"* (2 Thessalonians 3:6). This measure was the last resort and was instituted to protect other members of the body from the influence of the member who had rejected all entreaties and counsel.

Paul made use of a very strong expression in his advice for dealing with moral doctrinal offenders. Concerning the moral offender, he said, *"To deliver such an one unto Satan for the destruction of the flesh, that the spirit may be saved in the day of the Lord Jesus"* (1 Corinthians 5:5). He dealt with two men who were guilty of overthrowing the faith of some in the same manner: *"Of whom Hymenaeus and Alexander; whom I have delivered unto Satan that they may learn not to blaspheme"* (1 Timothy 1:20). Perhaps the expression refers to exclusion from the church and turning people over to Satan for chastisement. This is unclear, but what is clear is that they were to be restored to church fellowship when they show signs of repentance: *"Sufficient to such a man is this punishment, which was inflicted of many. So that contrariwise ye ought rather to forgive him, and comfort him, lest perhaps such a one should be swallowed up with overmuch sorrow"* (2 Corinthians 2:6–7).

The restoration of healthy discipline is one of the great needs in the churches today. Men and women commit all kinds of sin and retain their membership in the churches. The witness of the church has been greatly hindered by its failure to deal with unworthy members.

In the Community

The church has a duty to the community of which it is a part. Its first duty is to seek to bring everyone within its reach to a saving knowledge of the Lord Jesus Christ. It is to hold high standards of conduct before the community. Unworthy living on the part of church members is a curse to any community. The church should also extend a helping hand to the needy in the community, whether the people who help are members of the church or not. Many have been won to Christ by the kind ministry of the church in times of distress and need. The church has a responsibility to look after the social needs of the community rather than leaving this field to the forces of evil. The enemy does not intend good to any man; we should be a ready people with a clear message, ready to rescue those around us and meet their needs.

In the World

Jesus said, *"The field is the world..."* (Matthew 13:38). The church has a world mission. Jesus did not leave it to the church to decide whether it would be a missionary or not. He decided that when He said, *"Go therefore and make disciples of all nations"* (Matthew 28:19, ESV). *"And ye shall be witnesses unto me both in Jerusalem, and in all Judaea, and in Samaria, and unto the uttermost part of the earth"* (Acts 1:8). There are three truths the church should understand.

Everyone Needs the Gospel

John gave us a terrible picture: *"The whole world lieth in wickedness,"* or in a more vivid translation, *"under the sway of the wicked one"* (1 John 5:19 NKJV). It is a lost world, and the gospel of Christ is its only hope. The good news is that the gospel is powerful and sufficient for the whole world. Jesus has entrusted His people, his church, with His message. It is a message that we are commissioned to bring to the entire world.

Again we have the testimony of John: *"And he is the propitiation* for our sings: and not ours only, but also for the sins of the whole world" (1 John 2:2). There will never be another Savior, because there will never be a need for another Savior. The atonement of Christ is sufficient for all the world.

"Go ye into all the world, and preach the gospel to every creature" (Mark 16:15). That is His only plan.

It is not only a lost world; it is a suffering world. There are multitudes without food and shelter. Wars and famine have left millions destitute. People are persecuted and slavery is still prevalent. The church cannot escape its responsibility to minister to a suffering world.

Public Ministry

Jesus commanded His disciples to go and preach. On the Day of Pentecost, when the church went forth under the power of the Holy Spirit, it was the public witness of Peter and the other disciples that brought the multitude to their knees in repentance. It was the public ministry of Paul and the other apostles and workers that stirred the hearts of the people all over the Roman Empire, and led to the establishment of churches in every population center. This was God's method of reaching men: "For after that in the wisdom of God the world by wisdom knew not God, it pleased God by the foolishness of preaching to save them that believe" (1 Corinthians 1:21).

There is no substitute for preaching the gospel. Several years ago, it was suggested in some quarters that there should be a moratorium on preaching. What a crazy idea! Perhaps there should be a moratorium on some preaching, but not on gospel preaching. It is God's method of making His message known—and it works just as well today as it did in the first century. The preaching of the gospel always produces results. Preaching is God's method to reach

His children, and every member of the church has a part to play in sharing the message.

Personal Work

Everyone was created for a unique purpose, so there is something for every member of the church to do. Not all are endowed alike, but each one has his or her own place to fill: *"Having then gifts differing according to the grace that is given to us, whether prophecy, let us prophesy according to the proportion of faith; or ministry, let us wait on our ministering: or he that teacheth, on teaching; or he that exhorteth, on exhortation: he that giveth, let him do it with simplicity; he that ruleth, with diligence; he that sheweth mercy, with cheerfulness"* (Romans 12:6–8).

There are people who will only receive Christ's message through one of us. One of the primary ways the enemy tries to bring down the body of Christ is through discouragement. He whispers in our ears that we aren't important or valuable and what we do is worthless because we are not pastors or teachers or another visible position in the church. This is a lie. Everyone we meet is a potential convert. We affect every circumstance, situation and person we meet for good or for ill. May God give us courage and wisdom and strength. The world is watching.

We are called by God to be His people and accomplish His

> There are people who will only receive Christ's message through one of us.

directives in our lives. There are three primary ways in which we can do this, and the early church modeled all three.

1. Being a Personal Witness

Every Christian should be a soul winner. This is not work for a few to do, but for all Christians. And everyone should prepare themselves to be the best soul winner possible. In the early church, all the members were witnesses for Christ: *"Therefore they that were scattered abroad went everywhere preaching the word"* (Acts 8:4). If Christians all through the centuries had maintained the zeal of the early Christians, there would not be millions of people in the world who have never heard the gospel.

There are several ways in which individual Christian can witness for Christ. Exemplary living comes first. Christians are to live so that others will *"take knowledge of them that they have been with Jesus."* People notice how we live, how we act, what choices we make. There is also the testimony of the lips. If one is a real Christian, he or she has something to say, and God expects him or her to say it. Letters and gospel tracts can also be used in winning others to the Savior. People who have God's passion for the lost in their souls will find a way to witness for Christ.

2. Prayer

The early Christians were mighty in prayer. There's an old saying that there will be more power in the pulpit when there is more prayer in the pews. There is much truth in that. Prayer undergirds the work of God. Spurgeon who was nicknamed the Prince of Preachers once said, "Among all the formative influences that go to make up a man honored of God in the ministry, I know of none more mighty than the intercession of his parishioners. Without it, he will most likely be a failure!" Pastors want their preaching to be clear and strong, meeting with faith in their hearers. That dynamic is the result of prayer.

The truly beautiful thing about prayer is that God leads us as we pray, so it's a partnership. We are led to pray according to His direction and we enjoy His presence at the same time. A win-win situation.

Some Christians are in circumstances that do not allow them to engage in the activities of the church. There are those who no longer go out because of age and/or physical infirmities. Prayer is an especially good option for them.

A story is told of a Christian girl who was deeply interested in missions and was constantly suggesting methods by which larger things could be accomplished. One day a friend said to her, "I believe that if you were put on an island alone, shut in a solitary cell, and debarred from communications with a solitary person, you would contrive to do something for missions."

"Certainly," replied the girl, "I would do the greatest thing possible for missions: I would pray."

3. Giving

Every Christian can help support the ministries of the church financially. Not all can go out as missionaries or become preachers, but they can contribute to make it possible for others to do so. And each one is to contribute according to his or her means: *"Let every one of you lay by him in store, as God hath prospered him"* (1 Corinthians 16:2).

Every Christian is a steward of God, and *"it is required in stewards that a man be found faithful"* (1 Corinthians 4:2). The people of Israel were required to take their tithes to the Lord: *"The*

139

tenth shall be holy unto the Lord" (Leviticus 27:32). Certainly no less than the tenth would be expected of Christians. Not only that, but as we are stewards of God, all we have is to be held in trust for God and used for His glory.

Cooperation in the Body of Christ

The church membership can do their best work only as they work together. Paul painted a beautiful picture of cooperation among the members of a church in his epistle to the Philippians: "If there be therefore any consolation in Christ, if any comfort of love, if any fellowship of the Spirit, if any bowels and mercies, Fulfil ye my joy, that ye be likeminded, having the same love, being of one accord, of one mind. Let nothing be done through strife or vainglory; but in lowliness of mind let each esteem other better than themselves. Look not every man on his own things, but every man also on the things of others" (Philippians 2:1–4). He rebuked the church at Corinth for the divisions and strife that existed among them, reminding them that they were *"God's fellow-workers"* (1 Corinthians 3:9, ASV).

> All we have is to be held in trust for God and used for His glory.

There must be cooperation among the churches. No single church, working alone, can adequately carry out the program of Jesus for the world. The churches must join together in a cooperative effort. There was cooperation among the churches in the New Testament era. While there was no definite organization, such as our conventions, Paul and his associates acted as a central committee through which the churches could pool their offerings for a common cause: *"But now I go unto Jerusalem to minister to the saints. For it hath pleased them of Macedonia and Achaia to make a certain contribution for the poor saints which are at Jerusalem"* (Romans 15:25–26).

"And we have sent with him the brother, whose praise is in the gospel throughout all the churches; And not that only, but who was also chosen of the churches to travel with us with this grace, which is administered by us to the glory of the same Lord, and declaration of your ready mind: avoiding this, that no man should blame us in this abundance which is administered by us: providing for honest things, not only in the sight of the Lord, but also in the sight of men" (2 Corinthians 8:18–21).

Paul looked on these common funds as a sacred trust that must be administered in a way that would leave no grounds for criticism. They were given for a definite purpose, and Paul and his associates had no authority to divert them to other causes, even if they wished to do so.

This, then, is God's plan for His work: His churches, free and independent, voluntarily entering into a cooperative effort for the promotion of their common causes.

STUDY QUESTIONS FOR CHAPTER EIGHT:
OUR MISSION

1. What was the work our Lord committed to the church?

2. The early church was exhorted to be a bulwark of the truth. A fortification not only protects, but is easily seen from a distance. How does the church guard and proclaim the truth today?

3. How should the body of Christ take care of its own needs?

4. How should offenses be handled within the body?

5. What serious issues require pastoral discipline? What is the protocol by which brethren are to be restored in the body?

6. As a leader, what have you learned about this aspect of church discipline that might help another leader?

7. How does the Great Commission work for you?

8. What are the three primary obligations of every Christian according to Dr. Scott? Take turns discussing each one.

9. If you are a leader, how can you encourage your congregation in these areas? If you are a layman, how can you support the growth of your church through these and possibly other ways?

10. Why is cooperation within the body vital? What things tear it down and how can you steer clear of these and personally edify the body instead?

Chapter 9

Our Victory

"U pon this rock I will build my church; and the gates of hell [Hades] shall not prevail against it" (Matthew 16:18, addition mine) is the emphatic statement and definite promise of Jesus. Other translations of these words have been given—for example, "The might of Hades shall not triumph over it" (WNT) and "The powers of death shall not prevail against it" (RSV).

The Hebrew word Sheol in the Old Testament has the same meaning as the Greek word Hades in the New Testament. They do not refer to the future place of torment; Gehenna is the word used for that. Gehenna originally referred to the Valley of Hinnom, a place outside the city of Jerusalem where Ahaz (and others) had sacrificed their children to pagan idols. Referring to Ahaz, the Bible says, "Moreover he burnt incense in the valley of the son of Hinnom, and burnt his children in the fire, after the abominations of the heathen whom the Lord had cast out before the children of Israel" (2 Chronicles 28:3). This evil place eventually became a garbage dump and was known to be a place of continual burning where worms ate and broke down what was thrown there. This is the place Jesus likened to hell; this area was known to all the disciples.

The words *Sheol* and *Hades* are sometimes translated as "death" or "the grave." A clue to their full meaning is found in several passages in the Old Testament: *"Have the gates of death [Sheol] been opened unto thee?"* (Job 38:17, addition mine).

"Thou that liftest me up from the gates of death [Sheol]..." (Psalm 9:13, addition mine).

"I shall go to the gates of the grave [Sheol]..." (Isaiah 38:10, addition mine).

The reference in these passages is plainly about the realm of death, the place where the immortal souls of mankind were kept. Gates are the means by which entrance is made. The gates of Hades refer to the entrance into Hades. The souls of men could not escape Sheol. The word translated "prevail" means to be strong against. It is found twice in the gospel of Luke: "Watch ye therefore, and pray always, that ye may be accounted worthy [prevail] to escape all these things that shall come to pass..." (Luke 21:36, addition mine).

"And the voices of them and of the chief priests prevailed" (Luke 23:23). The word seems to carry the idea of gaining the victory.

The Gates of Hades Shall Not Gain the Victory!

Scripture says this about the church: *"...and the gates of hell shall not prevail against it"* (Matthew 16:18b). Several interpretations of this passage have been given. Some think it points to the resurrection of the saints: *"Death will not be able to hold my church. My redeemed shall rise again."* Others interpret it to refer to the resurrection of Christ: *"The ecclesia is built upon the Messiahship of her master, and death, the gates of Hades, will not prevail against*

144

her by keeping Him imprisoned," says author Alan Hugh McNeile. *"The gates of Hades or bars of Sheol will not close down on it. Christ will rise and keep His church alive,"* Robertson states.

A third view is that death will not be able to destroy the church. Its gates will never open and swallow up the church. There will always be a church. This is not a promise of perpetuity to any particular church, but of the church as a whole. There will always be churches in the world.

Whichever view we adopt, we do realize that Jesus' death and resurrection effected great change in this area. No longer would people have to live in bondage to the fear of death. Instead believers could look forward with assurance.

Once Jesus conquered death, He emptied Sheol of His own. Peter preached just after Pentecost that *"every soul that does not listen to that prophet shall be destroyed from the people"* (Acts 4:23), which agrees with the words of Jesus that He came to save mankind and that only those who rejected Him would be condemned (John 3:17,18). Henceforth the redeemed would (as Jesus taught) pass *"from death to life"* (John 5:24 RSV). Clearly believers who had accepted Jesus as their Savior now had entrance to the throne room of God, while those who rejected Jesus had made a choice to live in eternal torment apart from the presence of the Lord.

THE CHURCH WILL HAVE ENEMIES

Because Christ instituted the church to carry on His work in the world, it was to be expected that Satan would seek to destroy it, just as he tried to destroy Christ when He was born.

First, Satan tried attacking the church from the outside. He hurled every weapon he could forge against it. He tried ridicule; he tried fire and sword; and he tried imprisonment and death. Christians were beaten and stoned, cast into prison, thrown to the wild beasts, burned at the stake, and nailed to crosses. But the hand of persecution could not destroy the church. It marched on from victory to victory.

Having failed in his efforts to destroy the church from the outside, the Devil tried a more subtle plan. He got on the inside of the church and began tearing it down from within. He was more successful in this. The church has never suffered defeat from the enemies on the outside. Every defeat it has ever known came from foes within.

Paul warned the elders of the church at Ephesus against both classes of enemies: *"For I know this, that after my departing shall grievous wolves enter in among you, not sparing the flock"* (Acts 20:29). Wolves do not belong to the flock; they are enemies from the outside that come in to destroy God's people..

Then the apostle continued, *"Also of your own selves shall men arise, speaking perverse things, to draw away disciples after them"* (Acts 20:30). The greatest danger was from within. The early church suffered from these enemies. What were some of them? We will look at four in detail.

Unbelief

For a time, unbelief encamped on the outside of the church and hurled its weapons of ridicule against it. But failing there, unbelief sneaked into the church and began its deadly work. Paul found unbelief at work in the churches he established: *"I marvel that ye are so soon removed from him that called you into the grace of Christ unto another gospel: which is not another; but there be some that trouble you, and would pervert the gospel of Christ"* (Galatians

1:6–7).

Similarly Peter warned those to whom he wrote, *"But there were false prophets also among the people, even as there shall be false teachers among you, who privily shall bring in damnable heresies, even denying the Lord that bought them"* (2 Peter 2:1).

Unbelief is still at work in the churches: unbelief concerning the very fundamentals of our faith, unbelief concerning the truth and authority of the Scriptures, unbelief concerning the person and work of Christ, unbelief that would pluck the diadem of deity from His brow and present Him to the world as a mere man and just another great teacher, unbelief that would tear the cross from the heart of the gospel and leave the world without a Savior, unbelief concerning the resurrection of Christ, unbelief that would leave His body in the grave and leave us with a dead Christ instead of a living Savior, unbelief concerning sin and salvation and the world to come. Unbelief is a big problem.

> # Unbelief is still at work in the churches.

Aside from the many forms of unbelief named above, we can have unbelief in our own hearts and minds of which we are unaware. Once we believe in Jesus, it is easy to go through the motions in church and not confront our own strongholds of unbelief. Sometimes we do not recognize that we make some of the choices we make because we are not believing and trusting in God. We can walk in our own strength and follow the dictates that seem right to us in our minds in ministry, especially if we are endowed with skills in that area. We can fail to draw from Christ in ministry if we are charismatic and easily loved too. Unbelief shows itself in us. If we feel fearful, worried, are controlling or critical, and go to prayer as a last resort, we probably have an undiagnosed problem in this area. This can be a big problem for those of us who are more independent too. We need to humble ourselves before God individually and hear from Him. We must allow the Holy Spirit to open our eyes to see unbelief in our hearts and minds. He is the only One who can minister to us and heal our hearts

Covetousness

The sin of covetousness found its way into the human heart in the very beginning. It blighted many lives. The last of the Ten Commandments deals with this sin: *"Thou shalt not covet..."* (Exodus 20:17). Jesus warned against it: *"Take heed, and beware of covetousness..."* (Luke 12:15). Yet covetousness soon found its way into the church. Judas, one of the Twelve, was moved by covetousness when he betrayed Jesus. It was one of the sins that brought the judgment of God upon Ananias and Sapphira. Paul called on the Colossians to turn away from covetousness, which he called idolatry: *"Covetousness, which is idolatry..."* (Colossians 3:5). He described the deadly effects of this sin in his first epistle to Timothy: *"For the love of money is the root of all evil: which while some coveted after, they have erred from the faith, and pierced themselves through with many sorrows"* (1 Timothy 6:10).

The sin of covetousness still finds a place in the church. It leads men and women to withhold the holy tenth from God and spend it on themselves. It hinders the progress of the church at home and abroad. It keeps many Christians from a full enjoyment of their Christian life. When we live a strong and healthy Christian life, pouring ourselves out for those around us and thinking of others first, we gain an abundant life here and now and forever. This is a win-win situation. The richness Christ brings to our soul cannot be

148

measured by worldly gain. Nothing the world supplies can match the joy and peace and love He brings to our lives.

Further the desire to be rich in worldly goods leads multitudes of people to put their hope and faith in all the wrong avenues, eventually leading to their complete ruin.

Worldliness

Worldliness is the antithesis of godliness. John described it when he said, *"For all that is in the world, the lust of the flesh, and the lust of the eyes, and the pride of life, is not of the Father, but is of the world"* (1 John 2:16). The early church was warned about these things: *"Be not conformed to this world..."* was Paul's exhortation to the church at Rome (Romans 12:2).

James, the Lord's brother, used this strong language: *"Know ye not that the friendship of the world is enmity with God?"* (James 4:4).

And John was equally emphatic in his condemnation: *"Love not the world, neither the things that are in the world. If any man love the world, the love of the Father is not in him"* (1 John 2:15). Some of those who had taken a leading part in Christian work went down in defeat because the world got too strong a hold on them.

> # Worldliness is the antithesis of godliness.

Demas was described as one of Paul's fellow laborers (Philemon 24), but he succumbed to the love of the world and deserted. *"For Demas hath forsaken me, having loved this present world..."* Paul wrote in his last message (2 Timothy 4:10).

Worldliness has always been one of the subtle enemies of the church, putting out the fires on the altar and hindering spiritual progress. Scottish churchman and songwriter Horatius Bonar said, *"I looked for the church and found it in the world; I looked for the world and found it in the church."* It is a sad day for the church when the line that marks it off from the world is blurred or obliterated. This is too often the case today. Only a return to holiness and being filled by the Lord daily can combat this insidious enemy.

Formalism

This evil seems not to have invaded the early churches to any great extent, but the danger of it was recognized even then. In what was perhaps his last letter, Paul described the conditions that would exist in the last times. He spoke of "perilous times" that would come. He gave a list of the signs of which men would be guilty. The last he mentioned was *"having a form of godliness, but denying the power thereof..."* (2 Timothy 3:5).

> Religion must have a form, just as the spirit must have a body.

Religion must have a form, just as the spirit must have a body. But just as the body without the spirit is dead, so religious form without the Spirit of power is an empty shell. It is closely akin to hypocrisy, a sin our Savior condemned severely. It is an evil that threatens the church of Christ today—form without power, organization without function, worship without life, and altars without fire.

Many churches have become social institutions, no longer preaching the gospel of Christ, no longer urging people of their need to be born again. Without a real conversion as our shared experience and a determination to allow the Holy Spirit His place in our churches, formalism waits for us. We must constantly be on guard against following Jesus out of duty and not desire. Jesus is the Lover of our souls and the undisputed Master and King of the Universe. May our churches reflect the One we serve.

SOME DEFEATS

Because the church is composed of imperfect men and women, there will be no perfect church on earth. The churches of the New Testament were far from perfect. There were divisions and strife in some; there was immorality; and some were guilty of lapses in doctrine. Among the seven churches of Asia, only one escaped severe condemnation from Christ in Revelation. The churches were not always victorious in their fight against evil, and they tasted defeat more than once.

Throughout the centuries, the church has suffered many defeats. It has been led astray by false doctrines; it has gone down before the forces of evil. There have been times when it seemed that the church had been swallowed up, that the gates of Hades had prevailed against it. But out of these experiences a revitalized church has risen to carry forward the work of Christ.

It is like a messenger who has been entrusted with an important message to carry through enemy territory. The enemy opens fire on him, and he is almost concealed by the smoke and dust. It looks as if he might have been killed. But when the smoke and dust have cleared away, the messenger is seen in the distance, speeding on with his message.

The church has been entrusted with the most important message the world has ever heard, and it has been commissioned to carry that message to the ends of the earth. The enemy has trained its guns on the church, and sometimes it has seemed to annihilate it. But the church has come forth with renewed strength and speeded on with its message. It has not been overcome.

The churches (assemblies) of today are not always victorious. Often they falter in the face of the foe. They have not laid aside every weight. Their progress has been impeded by the sin that so easily besets them. They have not always kept their eyes on Jesus Christ, the Author and Finisher of their faith. Yet it is to the church that men turn for help in time of need. It is the church which still holds the answers to every problem men face today.

TRIUMPH IN THE END

Although the church has been often defeated, and sometimes appeared to be on the verge of destruction, it has always emerged with new life and power. The enemies of Christ nailed Him to a cross, saw His body buried in a tomb, and thought they were rid of Him forever. But on the third day, they were startled by the tidings that He was alive and walking again among men. About the eighteenth century, men like David Hume, the Scottish philosopher and historian, were predicting that Christianity would be dead by the end of the century. But before that century ended, a great revival under Wesley and Whitefield swept over England and America and regions beyond, kindling religious fires that are still burning. In France, Voltaire and his unbelieving associates declared that Christianity was dead and that Christian temples would soon be changed into halls of science. But at that same time William Carey emerged from England and started a missionary movement that was to sweep the entire earth.

There are those today who say the church has failed, and we must look to something else. Many institutions called churches have failed, but the true church of Christ will never fail. Its ultimate victory is assured by several factors.

Christ: the Divine Builder.

It was Christ who said, *"Upon this rock I will build my church."* If it had been built by men, it would have been defeat long ago. But Christ built it, and He built it on a rock that will not crumble. It was said of Abraham that *"he looked for a city which hath foundations, whose builder and maker is God"* (Hebrews 11:10). That may be said of the church. It has foundations, and its Builder and Maker is Christ.

Some people are still saying, *"The church is failing and will pass away."* But the living Lord steps into the midst of the doubts and fears and says, *"No, the church will not fail. I built it; I know what went into it, and I poured into it the agony and sorrow of Gethsemane, the suffering and death of the cross, the glory of the resurrection, and the power of Pentecost. It will not, it cannot, fail."* When you feel overwhelmed by the bad news around you (even in the church), trust the Builder.

His Divine Presence

Recall the words of Paul to the church at Corinth: *"Know ye not that ye are the temple of God, and that the Spirit of God dwelleth in you?"* (1 Corinthians 3:16). This was the assurance of victory that John gave to the church of his day: *"Greater is he that is in you, than he that is in the world"* (1 John 4:4). With a presence like that within it, the church will not fall before its enemies.

His Divine Promise

We are part of a large family, and Jesus' promises have been given to each of us. Many Christians can attest to the fact that the Word of God is quickened to them by the Holy Spirit when they are in need of direction, reassurance, comfort, wisdom, and many other instances. Many can also point to a group of verses that they have claimed as life verses because the Holy Spirit has whispered them in their ears numerous times in their lives. Unlike other books, the Bible creates deposits from which we can draw strength and help. The Word is sown in us and bears fruit. That's why the promises of God are so very important. We can hold onto them in the face of any trial, knowing that *"every word of God proves true; he is a shield to those who take refuge in him"* (Proverbs 30:5).

It was Jesus Christ our Lord who said, "The gates of Hades shall not prevail against it." That promise of our Lord will not fail. Whatever experiences the church must pass through, and however powerful may be the foes arrayed against it, there will be victory in the end.

HIS BODY TODAY

Being part of the body of Christ is no small thing. We are called and chosen for a reason. It is well to emphasize two key points.

Our Responsibility

Church membership should never be taken lightly. It means something to be a member of the church of Christ. First it requires a conversion experience in which the new member can point to a time in which they submitted themselves to God and believed in Jesus as their Lord and Savior. This is vital. We cannot give what we have not received. Only one who has received the Holy Spirit through conversion can truly be a member of the body of Christ.

Church membership carries with it high privileges and holy responsibilities. Those who are members of the church should enter into these privileges and accept these responsibilities. Joining a body of believers is a commitment to Christ Himself. It involves working together with others to advance the gospel, as well as actively taking part in discipleship. This requires "drawing from the well" personally. Only someone with a personal relationship with Jesus can successfully shoulder these responsibilities, and only that person will appreciate the true fellowship and ministry opportunities that church membership provides.

> We should search our heart and seek the will of God before uniting with the church.

Some want the privileges of church membership without the responsibilities. They want what the church can give, but refuse to carry their part of the load. Others care for neither the privileges nor the responsibilities. Their names are on a church roll, and that is about all church membership means to them. Neither of these extremes is healthy. Neither is acceptable.

We should search our heart and seek the will of God before uniting with the church. It means infinitely more than entering one's name on a membership list. At the same time, the church should exercise great care and watchfulness in receiving members. Godly and Godward members are a must.

Only the Best

A certain business institution had this motto on its walls: *"Only the best is good enough."* That is truer of the church than any other institution—only the best is good enough for Jesus. Some seem to think that anything is good enough for the church. They give the church the scraps that are left over. They spend their money on luxuries and give a pittance to the church. They are too busy to enter into the work to which the church is committed, and too distracted to notice the needs around them. Their time, that very precious commodity, is completely given to their own entertainment and pursuits.

> The time has come to make numbers count.

Studies show that only ten percent of today's church members can be counted on for any real sacrificial service. Thus, it's often the case that ten percent of the people do ninety percent of the work! Imagine if you had an army going forward to battle with only ten percent of its soldiers in line. What would be your hope of winning that battle? Sadly, very little.

Christ has called us to partner with Him in His continuing mission: the salvation and discipleship of all people. As a body, this requires us to live counterculture, not worldly lives. We are to pick up our cross daily and walk in obedience to Jesus' individual callings on our lives. Some Christians think this work is for the leaders of the church only. This does not agree with the word of God that urges us to "be imitators of God, as beloved children. And walk in love, as

Christ loved us and gave himself up for us, a fragrant offering and sacrifice to God" (Ephesians 5:1,2 RSV). This appeal is to every believer, not just leaders. Each of us has a work to accomplish in the Lord.

Too often the church has touted its burgeoning members and judged its success on its membership. Some people even think it is the goal of the church to fill a large building, but it's not. It's to glorify God and be a blessing to all the families on the earth giving Him our very best. We have taken great pride in counting numbers; the time has come to make numbers count.

STUDY QUESTIONS FOR CHAPTER NINE:
OUR VICTORY

1. Discuss the concepts of Sheol and Gehenna. What is the difference between the two terms?

2. The church has never suffered defeat from the outside. In what ways has the Devil been able to attack the church from within?

3. What forms of unbelief do you see at work in the church today?

4. What unbelief have you dealt with in your own heart?

5. In what ways does the love of money hurt the church today?

6. How has worldliness hindered the church? How does this cultural warfare affect you personally?

7. Paul warned about a time when we would have to deal with "having a form of godliness, but denying the power thereof..." (2 Timothy 3:5). What is the effect of this today? How can we combat it?

8. Discuss the effect of false doctrine on the church today?

9. In the end, our victory depends on Jesus Christ and His promises, those "exceeding great and precious promises" (2 Peter 1:4). He is the Architect, Builder, and Head of the church. Take some time to share the personal promises God has quickened to you from Scripture.

10. What process should be used to usher people in as members? How does their success relate to them being properly birthed?

11. How has the idea of a separation between clergy and laity in the church hindered it?

12. Consider your own personal calling. If you know what you are called to do, are you doing it? (If not, speak to others about how to accomplish that.) If you are, what encouragement can you give to others about this?

Epilogue

The church's destiny is tied to its foundation. If the church is built according to the blueprint found in Scripture with Christ as its cornerstone and the prophets and apostles as its foundation (Ephesians 2:20), it will stand. It will be victorious over every cultural assault. Its blood-bought believers will proclaim their deliverance from sin, the flesh and the Devil's plans for them; and they will be heard by the next generation. In Deuteronomy 28, God warned the Israelites to take the path of obedience. There is an urgency in the Spirit today for a return to the pattern given by God for the church. It's simple. Disobedience will lead to further compromise. Obedience to His Word will bring forth good fruit which glorifies our Father. We need to make a conscious effort to live authentic Christian lives that reflect our personal relationship with our Savior. As He died for us, we must needs die for those around us by laying down our lives and serving others with the heart of compassion we can access only through our Lord.

God's blueprint is alive. It is not man's version of a stale form of religion according to his or her own understanding of an ancient text. God's blueprint for us was always meant to have as its focus this incredibly wonderful and highly personal relationship with the Creator who drew up the plans in the first place. When we look at the church today, we are tempted to think it is splintered and beyond help, but that simply is not true. The One who holds all things together is still in charge of it. Jesus is not shocked by our present state, and never will be. He knows the way to lead us. As always, that way is a return to His original plan. Jesus is still working on plan A. He did not make a revision. We, as His church, have all the answers to the problems in the world today. We hold His plans in our hands and we know how to read them. May we all walk in obedience to His voice in our lives that says, *"…this is the way, walk ye in it"* (Isaiah 30:21).

References

Carroll, B. H., and J. B. Cranfill. An interpretation of the English Bible. Nashville: Broadman Press, 1947.

González, Justo L. The Story of Christianity. Peabody, MA: Prince Press, 1999.

Gundry, Robert H. A Survey of the New Testament: Fifth Edition. Grand Rapids, Michigan: Zondervan, 2012.

Henry, Matthew. Matthew Henry's concise commentary on the whole Bible. Nashville: Thomas Nelson, Inc., 1997.

The International Standard Bible Encyclopedia, Vol. 1: A–D. Grand Rapids, Michigan: William B. Eerdmans Publishing Company, 1995.

The International Standard Bible Encyclopedia, Vol. 3: K–P. Grand Rapids, Michigan: William B. Eerdmans Publishing Company, 1995.

Lawrence, and Robert J. Edmonson. Practicing the Presence of God. Westwood, NJ: Fleming H. Revell, 1958.

Ludwig, Charles. Cities in New Testament Times. Accent Books, 1976.

Maclaren, Alexander. Expositions of Holy Scripture. Grand Rapids, MI: W.B. Eerdmans Pub. Co., 1944.

MacNeile, Alan Hugh. The Gospel according to St. Matthew. London: St. Martin's Press, 1955.

Meyer, Carl S. The Church: From Pentecost to the Present. Chicago:

Moody Press, 1969.

Miller, J. R. When the song begins. New York: Thomas Y. Crowell, 1905.

Morgan, G. Campbell. The Gospel According to Matthew. Ada, Michigan: Fleming H. Revell Co., 1986.

Robertson, Archibald Thomas. A. T. Robertson's Word Pictures in the New Testament, six volumes. Nashville, TN: Broadman, 1930.

Strong, Augustus Hopkins. Systematic Theology. Seattle: CreateSpace Independent Publishing Platform, 2014.

Tasher, R. V. G. The Gospel According to St. Matthew: An Introduction and Commentary. Grand Rapids, Michigan: William B. Eerdmans Publishing Company, 1962.

About the Author

D r. Alphonso Scott was born in 1937 in St. Louis, Missouri. He is the son of the late Bishop Phillip Lee and Louvenia Scott. As a young child, he accepted Jesus Christ as his Savior and was baptized in the name of the Lord Jesus Christ. His elementary and secondary education began in the St. Louis Public Schools.

While the organist at the church of his father, Lively Stone Church of God, Dr. Scott enlisted in the United States Air Force. While serving his country, the Lord blessed him and he was awarded the Distinguished Flying Cross for Heroism, crediting him for saving forty-three lives. He also received five Air Medals for combat flying and two Air Force Commendations for excellent work performance.

In 1962, Dr. Scott was called into the ministry and preached his trial sermon in Mashbee, Massachusetts, in April 1963.

Upon retirement from the US Air Force in 1974, Dr. Scott accepted the pastorate of the Lively Stone Church of God in Nortonville, Kentucky. During that time, he served as chairman of the Ministerial Association in Nortonville, Kentucky, as chairman of the Ministerial Counselor Association of Hopkins County, Kentucky, and as a Commission Colonel for the state of Kentucky. He also taught in the Kentucky Public Schools for seven years.

Dr. Scott has attended San Antonio College, Merced College, and the University of Evansville, from which he earned a bachelor of liberal studies degree and a master's degree. He also holds a doctorate degree in pastoral ministry from Trinity Theological Seminary.

Recently, Dr. Scott was installed pastor of the Lively Stone Church of God in St. Louis, Missouri. He and his wife, the former Phyllis Boyd, are the parents of two sons, Dwight and Lee.

BUILD, GROW, SUSTAIN

If you believe in the message of this book and would like to share in the ministry of getting this important message out, please consider taking a part by:

- Writing about *Blueprint* on your blog, Twitter and Facebook page.

- Suggesting *Blueprint* to friends and encouraging them to visit the website: livelystone.org.

- When you're in a bookstore, ask them if they carry the book. The book is available through all major distributors, so any bookstore that does not have it in stock can easily order it.

- Writing a positive review on www.amazon.com.

- Purchasing additional copies to give away as gifts.

OTHER PUBLISHED TITLES BY BISHOP ALPHONSO SCOTT

You can order your copy through amazon.com

WWW.LIVELYSTONE.ORG